AF896129

"Three books in one, this highly original work full of recipes and culinary wisdom from Iran, Mexico, and the United States is as big-hearted, curious, and wise as Sara and Edgar themselves. I can't wait for you to cook from it."

—**HUNTER LEWIS,**
editor in chief of *Food & Wine*

"*Nixta Taqueria Presents: From Tacos to Tahdig* is a heartfelt reflection of Sara Mardanbigi and chef Edgar Rico's shared heritage, blending Mexican masa and Persian tahdig into a singular culinary narrative. More than a cookbook, it explores identity, culture, and the way food connects people across borders—capturing the same spirit of creativity and community that defines Nixta Taqueria."

—**CHINTAN KIRAN PANDYA,**
chef and founder of Unapologetic Foods

"This book is exactly what you feel when you walk into Nixta Taqueria: warmth, creativity, and deep respect for where food comes from and who it brings together. Every page feels like an invitation—to gather, to listen, to be human. More than a generous collection of recipes, *Nixta Taqueria Presents: From Tacos to Tahdig* is joyful and rooted in a genuine care for serving others, full of the kind of magic that happens when people come together to nourish. You can feel the intention on every page. This is food—and a book—made in service of connection."

—**ADRIENE MISHLER,**
actor, writer, and global yoga teacher

For my Mamani, Agha Joon, Baba Joon,
Mamani Fakhri, and the Persian ancestors
whose stories live within me.

Desde México, para el mundo.

NIXTA TAQUERIA PRESENTS

FROM TACOS TO TAHDIG

SARA MARDANBIGI AND EDGAR RICO
WITH JJ GOODE

PHOTOGRAPHS BY MACKENZIE SMITH

TEN SPEED PRESS
California | New York

NIXTA TAQUERIA PRESENTS

FROM TACOS TO Tahdig

RECIPES AND STORIES FROM MEXICO, IRAN, AND THE IN-BETWEEN

CONTENTS

MEXICO

Recipes from the Motherland

SALSAS, PICKLES, DRINKS, AND STUFF

IRAN

WHEN RICO MET BIGI

HOWDY, I'M EDGAR. And I was just a Mexican-American dude from Los Angeles with a dream, until I visited the Corn Doctor.

After working in restaurants in LA for almost ten years—at Craft, Son of a Gun, Trois Mec, and Sqirl—I set my sights on Austin, Texas, with a plan to open a taqueria. I loved the city's low-key vibe, affordable rents, and relative lack of red tape. And I loved the fact that it was a taco town. Even more so than LA. Don't get me wrong. People in LA love tacos, but they wake up and eat breakfast burritos. Austin is breakfast taco country—people there eat tacos from morning to night.

But slinging tacos was just a glimmer of an idea. About the important matters—you know, the what, the how, and the where—I had no clue. You can't just roll into taco town, open a taqueria, and expect to get butts in seats.

So, I set out on a trip to Mexico to get inspired. It was the first trip to Mexico I took by myself, a meandering six-month adventure that started in the northern state of Monterrey, wended through San Luis Potosí, where my parents were born, and ended at the tip of the Yucatán. I stayed with family, old friends, and friends I made along the way, including some very spirited abuelas. I ate tacos of all kinds and in all forms—from carne asada in the north to al pastor in Mexico City to tacos de cochinita pibil in Merida. In Mexico, tacos can be filled with, well, anything. Pig ear. Cow head. Corn fungus. Rice with hard-boiled egg.

I didn't have that aha moment until I hung out with my uncle Javier, who introduced me to the Corn Doctor, a "relative" of ours (in Mexican terms). I don't remember his name, but the man has a PhD in corn science from Tecnológico de Monterrey, the Harvard of Mexico. So we just call him the Corn Doctor.

I met up with him on the Michoacán leg of my trip in the city of Morelia, where he lived. I mentioned to the Corn Doctor that one of my favorite things about the tacos in Mexico was the tortillas, how they were so different from those in the US, the way they were earthy and left traces of their intoxicating aroma on your fingers. His eyes lit up. "I want to show you something," he said.

A two-hour drive later, we were bumping along the single dirt road that runs through a sleepy village in the foothills outside Uruapan. Uruapan is a famed hub of exceptional carnitas, but I soon learned we weren't here for pork.

Whenever he spotted anyone on the road, he'd roll down his car window and ask for Juan (I actually don't remember his name, but tbh, it was probably Juan.). And despite the common name, people always seemed to know exactly who he was talking about. "He went that way," they'd say, or "I just saw him over there." Eventually, we found him, riding a horse and wearing the kind of wide-brimmed hat I saw on cowboys in Texas. He greeted the Corn Doctor warmly and invited us to his home to see his cornfield. After all the incredible sights on my trip—the heaps of barbacoa, the pots of guisados—this seemed about as exciting as visiting an LA restaurant supply store. A cornfield is a cornfield. What's to see?

Juan took us around the back of his small house, but all I saw was a weedy jungle. Oh boy, I thought, a two-hour drive for this? Then I looked closer. Much of the foliage wasn't weeds at all but vines and bushes bearing squashes and beans. Here and there throughout the jungle were green stalks with small ears. The Corn Doctor led me into the thicket, grabbed an ear, and pulled back the husk to reveal kernels of a deep purple color. Another cob had kernels that were fire-engine red, and another had kernels of both colors and every shade in between.

This corn was grown from seeds with ancient ancestry, a far cry from the GMO corn grown from Roundup-Ready seeds that now dominates the globe. Yet it wasn't just Juan's corn that had caught the attention of people like the Corn Doctor. They were also enamored of his dirt. For 150 years, his family had been growing vegetables on this land according to the milpa standard, an old system of agriculture where farmers grow certain crops in close proximity (specifically, "the three sisters": corn, squash, and beans) to take advantage of their symbiosis.

That night, we ate dinner with Juan and his family. His wife made chicharrón stewed in salsa verde and a big pot of beans topped with nata, the thick cream skimmed off boiled milk from their one dairy cow. On the side was a stack of steamy, rainbow-colored tortillas—some purplish, some chocolate brown, some blue, some yellow. These tortillas were made right here, from the corn I'd seen earlier. For weeks the kernels had dried in the sun, then been boiled in a mixture of water and cal (calcium hydroxide), washed to remove some of the hulls of those kernels, and ground using a hand-cranked mill into a dough called masa. As we chatted before dinner, we watched his wife press the masa into rounds and cook them on a comal (a circular griddle) until they blistered and puffed. One taste and I was all in.

These tortillas also had weight, both literal and figurative. The process by which corn becomes masa, known as nixtamalization, was invented millennia ago in some small village by the Mexica people. It transformed the barely digestible grain into a nutritious product that sustained civilizations and nourished my ancestors. Without that Vitamina T, as we call the tortilla and the innumerable other shaped foods formed from masa that start with "t" (tlayudas, tetelas, tostadas . . .), my Mexican ass probably wouldn't be here. The corn that Juan and his family grew and used was heirloom, so these tortillas likely tasted like those my great-great-great-grandparents ate. I felt connected and inspired. A switch flipped. My vision of the taqueria came into focus.

I would use corn like this to make tortillas like this. They would be the delicious canvas, the foundation, the link to the past. Corn, nixtamal, tortillas—they were a part of my history I could touch. Yet as the son of immigrants, I grew up removed from my roots. That, too, shaped me into the man and cook I am today. What I'd serve on top of those tortillas would express this part of me—the Sqirl and Trois Mec alum, the creative, farmers' market–trawling, California-bred, newly minted Tejano.

Finally, I knew the What. Next up was the How.

HEY, I'M SARA. And I'm just an Iranian-American gal who's pretty good at a lot of stuff. I was in Austin minding my own damn business until I met this foo' named Edgar Ulysses Rico.

While Edgar was traipsing around Mexico having a torrid affair with corn, I was in Texas busting my ass and occasionally setting tablecloths on fire. I'd lived in Austin for more than a decade, doing a little bit of this and a little bit of that.

I worked in international education, placing students in study-abroad programs, traveling the world to help guide them, and occasionally being chased by a pack of saguis monkeys with tufts of gray hair sprouting from their ears. I helped build a local taco shop into an empire, which involved both talent acquisition and setting up a taco cannon and pimped-out taco truck complete with lasers and a fog machine. And I did event coordination for a big catering outfit, where we once did forty-eight events in four days. Maybe that's why during one of those to-dos, I lost track of the sternos and had to bust out the fire extinguisher.

I love it here in the capital of Texas, a city that feels like a town. With its warm people and hospitality, Austin reminds me of a cross between the northwest Arkansas town in the Ozarks where I grew up, and Iran, the country of my maman (mom) and mamani (grandma).

Edgar's aha moment came from corn. Mine came from rice. I've never met a rice doctor, but the matriarchs in my family might as well have PhDs in the subject. The joke in my family is that I am my mamani. We shared not only hammerhead thumbs and a silent cackle when something really tickles our funny bones, but also an insatiable appetite for rice.

Mamani was highly skilled in the kitchen, but it's my maman who—sorry, Edgar—is the greatest cook I've ever known. Her stew game is strong, but her claim to fame is her rice. Maman's was next-level fluffy. If decent Persian rice is a standard poodle, Maman's is a Pomeranian. Making Maman-level rice, as I was reminded often by my entire family, was the kind of skill that could get you a husband. Now, I can make some seriously good rice, but not because I'm thirsty for a proposal. I chose Edgar at least in part because I knew he'd still have me even if my rice was shit.

Maman is the GOAT of the kitchen, but my whole family is wildly, aggressively hospitable. Even my khaleh (aunt) Azam, whom my mom teases relentlessly for her mushy rice, is the queen of making you feel welcome, always. All those invitations, the come-in-and-eats, the lavishing of time, attention, and care on others—it shaped me. It's why I went into hospitality in the first place. I'm no pro cook, but I love to feed people, to bring them the kind of joy Maman delivered with a pot of rice.

Some day, I wanted to open a place where I could do just that. At this point, I understood the process: the staffing, the promo, the money stuff (finance major over here!). I knew the How but not the What. Edgar knew the What but not the How.

Then, one fateful evening, Gargar met Sasa, Rico met Bigi.

Before there were nicknames, Edgar and I spent a serendipitous week together at a catering gig—his first week and my last. After our final shift together, our whole crew ended up at Shangri-La, a classic Eastside bar, and over Fire Eagle IPAs, he and I both started feeling some type of way. I was taken by his LA swag, his retro Jordans, and kind-eyed baby face—the kind that makes actual babies stare, perplexed at how a gigantic man could have their exact face. He thirsted after my dad jokes and Mardanbigi sass. In the aftermath, he asked a mutual friend for my number and I returned his affections, like a good millennial, by sliding into his DMs.

The matriarchs and Gargar making tortillas on Nixta's plancha for the very first time.

Mamani and her lil' Bigi quartet at the Taylor House.

The Nixta Portal.

Sasa and Gargar's first dinner gathering: French Noir 2017.

Our first date culminated with us tossing around a tiny, rubber pig in some kind of hillbilly game I had never heard of. Our fifth ended in my room with us listening to the *Amélie* soundtrack on my phone and talking through the night. I got that feeling deep in the pit of my stomach. "I think I love you," I said. "I think I love you," he said. As the sun came up, I sheepishly informed him that I had to leave to drive the nine hours back to Arkansas for Thanksgiving. Don't worry, I took a power nap at a sketchy gas station.

And sometimes, when two people love each other very much, they decide to come together to bring a spot of brightness into this dark world. That's when the idea for Nixta was born.

HOLA + SALAAM, WE'RE NIXTA. Opening a business is a lot like having a baby. When Andrea, the owner of the cafe down the block from our house, mentioned she wasn't renewing her lease, we jumped. Edgar quit his job and turned my old Corolla into a small-bill ATM by driving for Uber and Lyft. I planned on being the pragmatic breadwinner who'd leave her job (with respectable notice) once the restaurant opened. Welp. Let's just say that a few months after we signed the lease, I no longer was. So we hustled, offsetting our rent and R&D costs by hosting Airbnb "Experiences" at our place.

Once your little business embryo seems viable, you spend a solid nine months being tested physically and emotionally. We stood on DMV-level lines in city buildings, waiting hours for our turn only to be told we were on the wrong floor. We haunted the offices of a certain city agency. We tried in vain to speak to a helpful human about licenses and permits. I almost got arrested outside another building, when after our umpteenth futile visit, I walked outside, flipped them the double-bird, and shouted, "FUCK Y'ALL!"

Then on October 5, 2019, we finally delivered. Inspections were passed. Gas was on. My brother, Mohamed, strung up some papel picados (those colorful Mexican paper decorations). Edgar's abuela Marta came armed with holy water to bless the building. During the fun, we made abuela one of our Tuna Tostadas (page 213). Mind you, she had never had tuna that wasn't from a can, let alone raw. She asked for another, and that made Edgar's day. When she complimented the tortillas, though, saying that she hadn't had one like it since Mexico, that made his whole damn life. That trip was the last time we'd ever see her.

An hour before we opened our doors, we noticed we had our first customer, Tim, camped outside on his lawn chair. Our menu was a manic, perfect reflection of Edgar's vision. The foundation of virtually every dish, from the tacos to the tostadas, was something ancient—masa, nixtamalized in house with heirloom corn from Oaxaca, Mexico, and North Texas. The topping for each glorious disc of masa, however, was pure first-generation American—right on the wavy line between past and present, tradition and innovation.

There was duck carnitas (see page 225), the pre-Hispanic protein of choice treated like the post-colonial pork preparation, where the meat is stewed then fried in its own fat. By a factor of five, it's been our top-seller from day one and every day since. It literally keeps our lights on. There were Enchiladas Potosinas (page 71), an homage to a dish from San Luis Potosí, the state in Mexico where Edgar's parents are from. We tucked duck-fat refried beans and chorizo-fortified potato puree inside warm guajillo chile–laced tortillas (in Spanish, enchilada just means "chile-fied") and topped it all with crunchy cabbage, salsa, and queso enchilado, which tastes like an extra-funky Parmigiano-Reggiano.

People liked us. All sorts of people, and a lot of them. More than we had ever expected and more than our 600-square-foot space could handle. That first day, in the brutal Austin heat, we had a line that snaked around the block for hours and hours. Good thing we'd hired a DJ and a little 1970s trailer slinging free margaritas.

Our first service was a hot mess. But our friends inhaled duck carnitas tacos and, abuela's new fave, tostadas crowned with raw tuna cured with citrus and tamari. Our neighbors scarfed versions of dishes they already loved—Edgar's Migas Tacos (page 190) are next level—and developed obsessions with dishes they had assumed they might not: Cauliflower Tacos (page 221) with romesco and pine nuts really do blow minds. A bona fide cowboy, in a wide-brim hat and copper-colored boots, crunched into one of our tostadas and proclaimed the topping to be "the best dang beef I've ever eaten." We gently informed him it wasn't beef but beet. "I feel bamboozled!" he erupted. "But I love it!"

No wonder my man won the James Beard Award and *Food & Wine* Best New Chef. No wonder he was on the *Time* 100 list and is a member of the State Department's culinary diplomatic corps. What else do you expect from a chef whose last name, Rico, means "delicious"?

And of course, there's the dish that got us a big-ass spread in the *New York Times* Dining section: "Sholeh Zard" (page 233). This Persian dessert is just rice pudding in the same way a Reuben is just a sandwich. I learned to make sholeh zard from Maman and when Edgar first had it, all he could think was, "Damn, this arroz con leche is fire." It has similar vibes, but what takes it to the next level is the perfume of cardamom and saffron, the surprising salty crunch of pistachios.

Of course, at Nixta, we first-genners did what we do best: bastardized the hell out of it, leaving a trail of enraged grandmas in our wake. We scaled back on the sweetness, left out the rose water, added a chingón amount of egg yolks and butter to make it super velvety, and finished it with pink powdered freeze-dried strawberries and flaky sea salt. People loved it. We loved that people loved it.

Almost as cool, though, was hearing the mix of English, Spanish, and Farsi from our team as they took orders and from customers as they placed them. It underscored the strange, amazing thing we had built.

When I sent the *Times* article that trumpeted the glory of our sholeh zard to Maman, she had two questions: First, what's the pink stuff in the picture? Second, what is the *New York Times*? She got most of her news from "In Session with Doctor Holakouee," a live call-in radio show where Persian moms phone in to complain about their underperforming kids. I genuinely believe she was unfamiliar with the newspaper. Edgar suspects Maman was making a statement. For Maman, after all, the entire notion of Nixta was a hard sell. She was afraid I was making the same mistakes Baba (that's my dad) had made.

Baba had also opened a restaurant after last-minute dropping out of his PhD program in agricultural engineering, for which he'd moved to Arkansas. It was called Friendly's and served American food with a few Persian dishes snuck in. After some good times and a few years, Friendly's didn't make it. Maman was worried that I was committing to a nearly impossible industry (in that, she wasn't exactly wrong) and sacrificing my independence by partnering with my husband.

It took Maman three years to come to Nixta. When she finally tried our sholeh zard, she pronounced it, "Different." (Lol.) At the end of her dinner, though, she looked at me and smiled. "You did good, Sasa Joon," she said. I'm not crying, you're crying.

THE BOOK

This book, like our business, is a celebration of where we came from and where we are. We're excited for y'all to come along for the ride.

For both of us, Nixta was our attempt at creating something that would make our parents proud, that took advantage of the opportunities they provided for us (sometimes at great cost) and also reflected the people we had become. In other words, we know all the nonsense our parents put up with just so we could fuck around and make duck carnitas tacos.

The typical line, one we've heard a million times and probably said a few times ourselves, goes something like this: I'm not Persian/Mexican enough for my family in Iran/Mexico and I'm not American enough for my friends in America. But that's not quite how we feel. We both feel accepted by our families and by our cultures. There are a few exceptions here and there, but that's how it always goes in family and culture. We're proud hyphenated Americans. We're happy in-betweeners. It's our superpower. We're able to call upon a rich culinary heritage when we cook. It inspires us but doesn't bind us.

All of it—our past, our present—deserves love. So, this book is divided into three major sections. First, there will be a chapter devoted to the dishes of Edgar's childhood in Visalia, California, of his family in Mexico. It will begin with the story of how he got here, plus a dip into masa, the soul of Nixta and the bridge between his heritage and home.

Next, it's Sara's turn to tell you about the magic of Maman, the glory of growing up with kuku sabzi and cheesy beans, and our epic trip to Iran. Then you'll find recipes from Sara's family and from our travels and learn the secrets to the fluffiest rice you've ever eaten.

The third chapter will focus on the so-very-American food served at Nixta, the strange and wonderful cuisine that takes shape when a Mexican-American guy joins forces with an Iranian-American gal.

Ándale and yallah—let's do this thing, friends.

The Mardanbigi-Rico clan celebrating our wedding in Mexico City at the legendary Contramar.

THE PANTRY

Here you'll find the ingredients in this book that deserve a little extra info. Some because they're unfamiliar to most cooks (hello, kashk) and others because we have a type or brand preference that we want to explain (hey, salt). And speaking of brands, note that when in doubt about Iranian products, look for the Sadaf brand. (Dior has Rihanna. Levi's has Beyoncé. And if they knew what was what, Sadaf would have Maman.) In the old days, we'd also tell you where to buy them. Nowadays, someone can probably bring you them all in 30 minutes or less (and you better leave a fat tip). Still, we're all about wandering the aisles of Mexican or Persian grocery stores.

AVOCADO, HASS

You know her. You love her. But you should probably let her ripen a little bit more, to experience her max flavor and creaminess. Hurry it along by keeping it in a closed paper bag.

If you want get a little fancy with your avocado slices—great for topping the tostadas in this book—try this: Halve and pit the avocado, then use a nice big spoon to scoop out the flesh in one big piece, starting at the wider end where the flesh meets the skin and following the curvature of the avocado. With the halves round-side up, thinly slice them lengthwise and nudge them with the flat of the knife to tip over the slices for a pretty fan effect.

BLACK LIMES

Persian cooking is big on sour flavors, and black limes is one of our aces in the hole. Cooked in salt water and then sun-dried, they can be dusky tan or nearly black and have an irreplaceable flavor—tangy, punchy, slightly astringent, and a little funky—that leaks into stews as the fruit bursts. Some people eat around them. Some greedily nibble them. You do you.

They're also labeled Omani limes (limoo Amani). If you can only find ground black lime, use 1 teaspoon ground for every 1 whole lime called for.

CANELA (MEXICAN CINNAMON)

Pale, more crumbly canela (aka Mexican, Ceylon, or "true" cinnamon) is milder with a warmer, sweeter aroma than the fossil-hard spice that's typically sold as cinnamon but is actually cassia. Both great spices, just different.

CARDAMOM

When we use cardamom in Persian cooking, it's the black pods, not the green ones, we reach for. Black shares some of the floral, warm, sweet flavors of green, but ups the ante with a bold smoky quality. If you must, swap in green, but don't tell Maman.

CHILES, FRESH AND DRIED

FRESH CHILES

Poblanos are mild (with a little kick if you're lucky), savory, earthy, and a little smoky, even before you char them. Jalapeños can be hot. Serranos are typically hotter and grassier—they're a fine sub for jalapeños and vice versa, but sometimes we insist on one or the other or a combo of both. Fresnos are moderately spicy and a lil' fruity. Habaneros are fire on the tongue and a fruity party in the nose. Clarification: When you sniff them, do not put the habaneros in your nose.

With hot fresh chiles, you can totally seed them to tone down the heat.

CREMA
SAFFRON
QUESOS
TOMATILLOS
SALT
CHILES
MEXICAN OREGANO
TURMERIC
TOMATO

CARDAMOM
AVOCADO
KASHK
MASIENDA
HEIRLOOM
WHITE CORN MASA HARINA
NIXTAMALIZED CORN FLOUR
GLUTEN-FREE
MASA HARINA
SAFFRON WATER
CANELA
FENUGREEK SEEDS
PILONCILLO
Sadaf
Special Blend Tea
with Cardamom Flavor
NET WT. 16 OZ (454g)
TEA

DRIED CHILES

Larger dried chiles have tons of dried fruit flavor and a little heat. Anchos are raisiny and sweet. Pasillas are, too, plus they have a smoky, earthy, chocolaty vibe. Guajillos have a little cranberry tartness. They're seedy, too, so often you'll be slitting them open, ditching the seeds, and closing them back up.

For smaller dried chiles, you keep the seeds in. They're hot and each has a distinctive flavor. Chipotles (the purplish morita variety for this book) are smoky and slightly sweet. Chiles de árbol are nutty. And teeny tiny chiltepínes are beguilingly citrusy.

CREMA

This Mexican product, with its tang and milky sweetness, is like drizzleable sour cream with even more fat. In a pinch, sub sour cream or crème fraîche mixed with just enough cream or milk to make it pourable.

FENUGREEK LEAVES

Maman is often busting out shambalileh (fenugreek leaves), fresh or dried depending on her access, for herb-crammed dishes like Kuku Sabzi ba Mahi (page 143) and Ghormeh Sabzi (page 156). They've got a slightly bitter and sweet, celery-tinged thing going, and there's really no substitute.

KASHK

This fermented yogurt product is a bit polarizing, because she's a bit intense. (She's also frequently labeled "liquid whey"—a bit confusingly, because she's thicc.) Fans, though, can't get enough, dolloping thick, tangy, salty, umami-funky kashk on their Halim Bademjoon (page 131) and Aush Reshteh (page 139). For this book, buy the jarred "liquid" kind that you'll find refrigerated at markets that stock Persian products.

LARD

When we call for lard, we mean the yellow-hued rendered pork fat you find at Mexican markets. The white lard sold elsewhere has less porky flavor, which is okay if that's your thing.

If you want, make it yourself: Buy a pound or so of pork fat, chop it into even 1-inch pieces, and add it to a medium heavy pot along with ¼ cup water. Bring to a simmer over medium heat and cook, stirring occasionally and adjusting the heat to keep the sizzle quiet, until the fat has rendered and is a little golden and slightly crispy, about 1 hour. Strain the lard into heatproof containers. Let the lard cool, then store in the fridge for up to 3 months.

MASA HARINA

It's masa (ground-up nixtamalized corn) but dried and pulverized. Do your cooking a favor and buy the good stuff that's cooked, dried, and ground in small batches from heirloom corn. For example, from the glorious company Masienda.

MEXICAN OREGANO

The flavor's a lot like the dried herb used in Mediterranean cooking, but with a whisper of anise and citrus. Shhh, it's not "true" oregano but a member of the verbena family. Double shhh, you can totally sub in standard oregano.

PILONCILLO

This unrefined brown sugar adds depth and an almost caramel quality to dishes. It comes as a hard cone, and you've got to bash or cut off chunks to use it. When shopping, make sure you get the real thing, peeping the ingredient list for any nonsense like corn syrup.

QUESO

France may try to claim the fromage territory, but Mexico has a serious cheese culture. In this book, you'll just be using three Mexican cheeses: mild, crumbly queso fresco; searable, unmeltable queso panela (cousin to Halloumi); and queso enchilado, chile-encrusted cheese aged for five years that hails from San Luis Potosí. For that last, harder-to-find cheese, Parm makes a decent sub.

SAFFRON

The world's most expensive (and Maman's most precious) spice for a reason. The next time you see a jar of tiny red saffron threads with a price that makes you blush, imagine vast fields of pale purple saffron crocuses. Each flower only has three threads (technically stigmas) and must be carefully plucked by hand, then dried and aged. For a pound of saffron, we're talking 68,000 flowers. Luckily, a little goes a long way. And when we say Maman is lavish in the use of her Iranian saffron, we mean she's going wild by using 1 teaspoon.

Buy high-quality saffron—a bargain usually indicates chicanery—and apply the following Persian technique for making saffron water (a sort of concentrate), which unlocks its warm, honeyed, floral aroma and flavor. Then you'll understand why the spice is more costly (pound for pound) than truffles or caviar.

SAFFRON WATER

Makes as much as you want

Use a small mortar to grind the saffron threads to a powder, then pour in hot water to bloom it. (Maman is particular but not precious, so feel free to do as she does and just microwave the water for 15 seconds or so.) Stir, let it cool, and it's good to go.

You can do it each time you need some (for every ¼ teaspoon saffron threads, use 1 tablespoon hot water) or use the same ratio (e.g., 2 teaspoons saffron, ½ cup hot water) to make a larger batch. It keeps in the fridge for up to 1 month.

SALT

Flaky sea salt, with those delicately crunchy flakes, is for that last-second sprinkle. For that, the Maldon brand is our fave. Kosher salt is for the rest of our seasoning needs. And for that, we like Morton and that's what we used to develop and test our recipes. If you choose Diamond Crystal kosher salt, however, use twice as much as we call for.

Many people prefer Diamond Crystal. We get it. We've even been shamed by certain people, including our friend and coauthor, for our choice, and you know what, we stand by it, JJ. For one, if you use Diamond instead of Morton, the worst thing that happens is you'll undersalt and have to add more later. The other way around would spell disaster. And second, Morton is based in Texas, after all, and we're nothing if not loyal.

TOMATILLOS

Mild-mannered and tart when raw, these husked green fruits turn tangy when roasted or boiled. When shopping, peek beneath the husks to make sure the fruits are mostly unblemished. When using, remove the husks and rinse well under running water, rubbing with your hands to remove the slightly sticky but totally natural stuff on the surface.

TOMATOES

Tomatoes are round red fruits that . . . Kidding, kidding. We just want to acknowledge that we use a lot of Roma tomatoes in this book. It's a type of plum tomato that's easy to find and has less moisture than many other varieties, making it great for sauces. Not a huge deal, though, so use whatever tomatoes look best.

TURMERIC, GROUND

This dried powdered root (okay, technically a rhizome) has a sunny, earthy, peppery vibe, and it flavors, oh, 99 percent of all Persian dishes. It contributes a beautiful yellow color to your dishes . . . and to your favorite white shirt (RIP to all white clothing).

TEA, TEA, SO MUCH TEA

In Iranian homes, hot tea steeping in a samovar greets you the moment you wake and just before bed. Specifically, Lahijan, a black tea from the region of the same name near the Caspian Sea, where my family has a tea farm. And more specifically, lab sooz, lab reez, lab dooz—so hot it scalds your lips, so brimming with tea that it reaches the lip of the cup, and so robust with tannic flavor as to seal your lips after sipping.

Like rice, the tea we offer is not just to enjoy but to show we care. The tea is both a sign of hospitality and its antidote—a few scalding cups helps wash away the agony of a glorious and punishingly generous Persian meal.

Also: When my siblings and I were young and had eye gunk that seemed to foretell an infection, Maman would pour tea in a saucer, dip a cotton ball in it, and swab our eyes. TMI? Always worked!

A FEW POINTS OF ORDER:

NO TEA BAGS. Grow up and steep loose tea leaves, preferably, long-leaf black Lahijan tea. The rule of thumb is 1 teaspoon leaves per guest, though you can go up and down based on preference.

NO MILK. Unless you're trying to piss off some Persians.

YES SUGAR, IF YOU WANT. You can go with a cube in the cup, but pros squirrel one away in their cheek and sip the tea as it slowly dissolves. Level up with a stirring-stick of saffron-infused rock sugar, which you can buy just about anywhere Persians flock.

NO EXCUSES. You are morally (and possibly even legally) bound to drink the tea that's served to you by your host.

NO MUGS. Have some dignity and refill a small cup, one without a handle so you exist in a constant state of silent pain.

Échale ganas, m'hijo.

Give it everything you got, my son.

—FLOR RICO (THAT'S MY MOM)

MEXICO

RECIPES FROM THE MOTHERLAND

$320
$200
$260
$280
$400
$275
#189
arnes Asadas
AIKO Y GABY
PRECIO POR KILO
TASAJO $ 320
CHORIZO $ 200
CECINA ENCHILADA $ 260
TRIPA $ 400
UBRE $ 280
COSTILLA ENCHILADA $ 280
PUESTO 188
PUESTO #187

CARNES AL CARBÓN
TASAJO $320
CHORIZO $200
CECINA $260
TRIPAS $400
$300
UBRE $280
$275
#201
PUESTO #202
MATY
PUESTO #202
Paquetes
$130
$195
$210
$275
$390
$550
$780

I GREW UP SMACK IN THE MIDDLE of California in a town called Visalia, the agricultural hub of America, baby. Hence the Mexicans of every sort, from everywhere—Veracruz to Baja, Oaxaca to Michoacán—all here to work.

My parents relocated there, some two hundred miles north, after the LA riots. Dad was a chef—kinda. Technically, he was a food scientist who made sure the food engineered at Starbucks and Taco Bell HQ was error-proofed for their minimum-wage hires. Mom went to dental hygienist school by day and cleaned at a food distribution warehouse by night. My grandma on my mom's side lived in nearby Salinas and worked the fields, picking (if I had to guess) heads of iceberg, cauliflower, and broccoli. Definitely broccoli. You could smell it in the air when you drove through Salinas with the windows down, that butt kind of smell.

Back then, there were two of me. Like a lot of immigrant kids, I had the Mexican me that kicked into effect at home. The one who spoke Spanglish, got dragged every Sunday to Our Lady of Guadalupe or something, and woke up to Dad's signature huevos con weenies, eggs scrambled with sliced hot dogs, plus chips or potatoes tossed in for texture. Whose fridge was packed with repurposed plastic containers holding beans or chicken tinga or pickled jalapeños. Cracking open one of those tubs was like playing Mexican roulette—like, oh snap, pozole! And then I had the American me, who rolled with the white boys at the "better" school Mom and Dad had hustled me a spot at. Who rocked with the Dallas Cowboys (my first brush with Texas); argued over who was better, Charizard or Blastoise, Barry Bonds or Mark McGwire; and fiended for his friends' Lunchables.

Sara once told me that, growing up, she had the urge to be anything other than "from somewhere else." Me, I wanted to be just one thing: American to the max. I remember this one summer I spent with my paternal grandma in Mexico, when I straight up refused to eat Mexican food. As a kid, I spent most summers in San Luis Potosí, the town where my dad grew up. Summers were when Mom would work extra hard to stack extra bread, and my sister and I would be shipped off. Classic immigrant shit. Abuela took my little tantrum in stride, patiently letting me drag her to eat burger after burger. Burgers were super American, I thought, with all that beef and ketchup and not a tortilla in sight.

Back in Cali, and in the presence of my parents' cooking, my embrace of chicken nuggets and pizza (that otherworldly quesadilla) was particularly weird, because what they made really was special. She and my dad switched off cooking, and he was no slouch. Dad was a griller and had some skills with carne asada and tablitas, beef ribs cut across the bone. He had a few simple stews in the repertoire, too, like chicharrónes (fried pork skins) simmered to jiggly goodness in salsa verde. Mom's bag of recipes was a little deeper, her ambitions a little grander, her seasoning a little more on point. She was the one who made mole, toasting chiles and frying nuts and fruit. She made tortillas, mixing water with masa harina (dehydrated pulverized corn), pressing and griddling each one, and serving us a steamy pile with dinner.

My whole Mexican food hang-up was funny. One minute, I'd be eye-rolling yet another pot of my mom's (legit incredible) carne ranchera—I don't think Sara ever scoffed at her maman's cooking—then the next minute my friends and I would be getting jacked up for our lunchroom's crispitos, a sorta Crunchwrap-looking burrito hybrid filled with ground beef and potato. Which, if we're being real, is pretty damn Mexican.

And looking back, so were all those burgers I insisted on eating in Mexico—topped with beans and crema and hot dogs. I mean, the vendors were straight up using tortilla presses to make the patties, squishing them razor thin like an early version of a Smashburger. They came with drinks served in plastic bags with the straw sticking out (if you know, you know). While my bias toward American stuff didn't always make sense, the meaning behind my preference was clear. I didn't want to be so hella Mexican, like my parents. I just wanted to be Edgar. Of course, the eye rolls weren't entirely sincere. I was trying my best to blend into American life. But like Michael Corleone, just when I thought I was out, Mexico pulled me back in.

Once in a while, we'd drive a few towns over to shop at El Progreso, a market run by my "uncle." My parents would always order Enchiladas Potosinas (page 71), named for the state in Mexico where they

DIA DE MUERTOS

were born. I probably complained that I wanted pizza, but I still ate those enchiladas with gusto. When we got home, I might have craved the thrill of meatloaf, but I also craved the comfort of my uncle's tortillas.

The ones from El Progeso just hit different. I didn't know why at the time, but they tasted like Mexico in a way my mom's tortillas just didn't. Later I learned why. My uncle didn't make them from masa harina, the kind of shortcut a working mom in a country that lacked molinos needed to get dinner on the table. Nah, he was making nixtamal and grinding it to make masa, just like they did at the local molino in San Luis Potosi. I didn't understand the alchemy (a process called nixtamalization) that turned corn from an unremarkable grain into a nutritious staple that sustained civilizations. I just knew it tasted like nothing else—the quiet, savory earthiness, and the slight mineral tinge of Mesoamerican science.

Life was like that for a while. I'd take five steps away from Mexican me, then one or two back. When I fell in love with cooking, for instance, I learned to cook sauce grenobloise, tuna tataki, and corn agnolotti—everything *but* Mexican food. On my days off, though, I'd be hitting up the taqueros on the streets of LA for everything from beef head to barbacoa to the mind-blowing tacos at Mariscos Jalisco, tortillas filled with some sort of crispy pureed shrimp (the details are still a family secret) and doused in spicy, soupy tomato salsa. I started to realize that no matter how far I delved into other cuisines, my palate, my entire being, would still be defined by the fragrances and flavors I grew up with—serranos and tomatillos charring on Mom's comal, the sweet, earthy waft from a pile of steamy tortillas.

When I finally left Cali in my late twenties, with a passionate but blurry vision for a restaurant, I took my big solo trip to Mexico. That's when I met the Corn Doctor in Michoacán and had my come-to-Quetzalcoatl moment: Nixtamalized corn, made by more or less the same process and with the same ingredients my ancestors used, offered a way to connect with the part of me I'd been running from. In order to move forward, I had to look back.

After that, I kept the learning going. I went to Oaxaca, the place where archaeologists suspect the tortilla was born more than three thousand years ago. I visited the cities and villages, markets and molinos, and asked everyone if I could watch them do their thing. No one said no. Instead, they welcomed my presence, this Cali-born gringo who spoke janky Spanish. Instead of swaggering young cooks in crisp whites, now my mentors were grandmothers, with the occasional grandson stepping in on abuela's day off.

Every operation was different. They used different field corn with kernels of kaleidoscopic colors—deep red and purple, pale blue and nearly black—either trucked into the markets or grown in jungly backyards a short stroll away. The kernels were boiled and then soaked, in stainless-steel vats or battered old pots, along with either purchased calcium hydroxide (aka cal) or homemade wood ash. Each was an option—one modern and one old-school—for creating the alkaline environment necessary to break down the kernels, unlocking their nutrients so our bodies can use them. This culinary innovation is what sustained the Olmec, Maya, Zapotec, and many others. Nixtamalized corn is so monumental an achievement that it holds a place in many creation stories. In Aztec mythology, for example, humans are legit made of masa—corn and life, inseparable.

After the corn was soaked, the mixture was ground—by motorized grinders in the cities, hand-cranked ones in the ranchos, and sometimes with a metate (a curved slab of volcanic stone) and temolote (a cylindrical pestle) for the true old heads. The resulting masa might be made into tamales and atoles (corn beverages!), not to mention tortillas, tlayudas, sopes, memelas, garnachas, gorditas, huaraches, and approximately a million other shapes made throughout Mexico that have earned names. (Spoiler alert: They're all more or less masa discs of different dimensions.)

In Mexico City, I showed up at the back door of Pujol, legendary chef Enrique Olvera's fine-dining restaurant. My offering to this culinary god was free labor in exchange for learning from a master. There, the cooks underscored that masa wasn't just a matter of chemistry. It was a craft honed over years of toil. The particulars of each crop of corn varied, and the masa maker had to develop instincts, ducking and weaving to calibrate the ideal ratio of starch content and alkali. At Pujol, masa was exalted, and only the most senior members of the kitchen brigade were entrusted with making tortillas. They worked with discipline and precision, mastery and pride—part Navy Seals and part artists.

While I got closer to my culture, I also had the good fortune of getting closer to a dope woman who has hammerhead thumbs and loves rice. And it was later through traveling to Mexico with her, before and after we opened Nixta, that accelerated my embrace of the full me.

I wanted to show her my way of traveling, so everywhere we went, I made sure we got the local specialty. I dragged her on a six-hour bus ride to Monterrey, in the north of Mexico, to eat cabrito (baby goat) and flour tortillas, translucent as stained glass. In Ensenada, it was fish tacos, ceviche, and Chenin Blanc from Valle de Guadalupe, and in nearby Puerto Nuevo, burritos crammed with spiny lobster.

We went to Mexico City, where we'd later get married, for all the suadero and al pastor and to ride the trajineras (colorful boats) along the canals of Xochimilco. The canals are remnants of massive bodies of water and a reminder that Mexico City, the sprawling metropolis of twenty-two million, began as a small island in Lake Texcoco.

In the Yucatán, I almost proposed to Sara on a hog farm, but that felt like a bit much even for a laid-back Muslim. Instead, we ate our weight in cochinita pibil—banana-leaf, achiote-rubbed blasphemy topped with electric-pink pickled onions. Then I almost proposed to Sara in a cornfield in Yaxcha, a Mayan village near the hog farm, but that was a bit too on-the-nose. (When we finally did get engaged, it was in the nearby city of Progreso, same as the name of the market in California. A sign!?)

We hit Oaxaca, the only state never colonized and therefore home to some of the most transporting, time-warpy food on the planet. We cruised Michoacán, the capital of carnitas, to devour pig parts—from snout to tail—cooked slowly in vats of lard. And for the first time, I came to San Luis Potosí with my boo. We shared a magical dinner with family, as intimate as a Persian affair, with a solid fifty cousins, aunts, and uncles there to welcome us. They even got us a gift, though they wouldn't outright tell us what it was. They led Sara and me to the backseat of some dude's car, and we warily surveyed a giant garbage bag wrapped with duct tape, about five feet long and, concerningly, warm. As Sara and I each heaved a side, we looked at each other like, What have we done?

Spoiler: It wasn't a body. It was a zacahuil, a jaw-droppingly massive tamale, coarsely ground nixtamalized corn mixed with a sauce of dried chiles, filled with various stewed meats and whole boiled eggs, and wrapped in banana leaves. Baked for nearly 12 hours and then spooned onto our plates, this regional dish was a glimpse into the past, into the culture of the Huastec people who lived here long before the Spanish came, with a texture reminiscent—at least to the two interlopers, both residents of the American South—of creamy grits.

Sara's presence made these trips especially revelatory, and not just because my girl is wicked smart. Showing her places and foods I knew so well along with experiencing the brand-new ones together clarified just how incredible Mexico is. How diverse (like a hundred different countries in one), how ancient and modern, how rich with history and stories, how delicious, and how welcoming.

Sara was particularly taken by the Mexican flavor of hospitality, which she described as so different from the hilariously aggro kind that would later charm me in Iran. Her favorite example was the time we pulled up to a hotel in Mexico City in our rented clunker with a sunroof that refused to close. The valet looked concerned. We were like, Whatever, we'll deal with it another time. The next day, we went to grab our car and, miraculously, the sunroof was fixed. The valet had called his mechanic cousin. Why? Just 'cause. For a long time, I had taken that kind of generosity for granted. Now, while Sara freaked at the gesture, I thought with pride, Yep, those are my people.

It's the pride for where I came from and the wisdom gifted to me by generous souls I met in my travels that I bring to Nixta, where, every dang day, we make masa. We get heirloom corn from farmers in Oaxaca and North Texas, typically a few varieties of whatever they're growing. Even though I've been in the game for a minute, each morning is a new experiment. Depending on what the corn brings us, we adjust the amount of cal and water. We tweak the next batch based on the first, how it feels in

our hands, how it looks after it's pressed to make tortillas, and how it eats once it's cooked.

I do it for my city, to share what brings me such joy. I want to make people happy, to serve the kind of tortillas you remember, to hit them with those vitamins and niacin, which aren't only great for your body but are great for your mood. I think tortillas are why Mexicans tend to be happy people. (Sara thinks the mezcal doesn't hurt.)

I also do it for me, not Mexican me and American me, which were always intertwined, but the me I've become. When I handle masa today, I feel like I'm working with something sacred, something that sustained my ancestors. When I make tortillas, I feel like I'm stepping back in time and paying homage to the people who shaped me long before I walked into that cornfield in Michoacán, long before my parents moved to America. I'm not crying, you're crying.

MASA AT HOME

Oh, right, this is a cookbook—I thought I was journaling. So now you're wondering, can you make masa at home? Absolutely! I mean, you'll need heirloom dried corn, calcium hydroxide, a hand-cranked molino or sixty-pound metate, and a whole lot of free time. If you're up for the task, allow me to introduce my boy (and Masienda founder) Jorge Gaviria's incredible book, *Masa,* where you'll learn how.

For this book, though, I'm going to suggest you buy fresh masa from the countless molinos—spots that turn corn into nixtamal and grind masa themselves—that have popped up all over the country. And if that fails, you're going to get some masa harina (dehydrated masa) and add water. It's called masa en la chinga—aka masa you make when you're in a rush (page 37). Preferably the magical masa harina from companies like Jorge's, which are made from nixtamalized heirloom corn. Or, if you must, you can totally buy the masa harina on offer at any grocery store nearby a city or town with a sizable Mexican population (aka just about everywhere). That's what Mom used back in the day. Call it gateway masa. Once you're hooked, maybe you'll try the good stuff.

Tito's
EL
Asesinos

CAFETERIA
tito's
BAGUETT
ANY
BBQ
Pregunta por ellos
tito's
tito's
PIÑA
CAPUCHINO
COCO
NANCHE
FRESA
DURAZNO
LIMON
GROSELLA
BESO DE ANGEL
NUEZ
VAINILLA
MANGO
OAXACA

TORTILLAS DE MAIZ

Corn Tortillas

You can make some banging tortillas, whether you buy fresh masa or rehydrate the dried stuff to make masa en la chinga—masa in a hurry. For more tortillas, just double, triple, and quadruple the ingredients.

Equipment: tortilla press and two 8-inch square or round pieces of plastic wrap

3½ cups (725g) fresh masa or Masa En La Chinga (recipe follows)

Makes about twenty-four 4 to 5-inch tortillas

Divide the dough into 24 equal portions (about 30 grams each) and roll into balls the size of a Ping-Pong ball. Transfer them to a tray and cover with a kitchen towel as you make the tortillas.

Heat a dry cast-iron skillet or comal over medium-low for 2 minutes. Increase the heat to medium.

Line the bottom plate of a tortilla press with an 8-inch square or round piece of plastic wrap. Put a dough ball in the center, use your fingers to press gently to flatten it slightly. Cover with the second 8-inch square or round piece of plastic wrap and close the tortilla press, pressing firmly but nothing crazy. Open, flip the tortilla (still sandwiched by the plastic), and press again. The goal is a tortilla that's an even 1⁄16 inch thick.

Open the press, gently peel back the top layer of plastic, then flop the tortilla onto your palm and peel off the remaining plastic. Hold the tortilla over the skillet and gently rotate your hand to lay the tortilla flat onto the hot surface.

Cook for about 20 seconds on the first side. Flip and cook for another 30 seconds, then flip once more and cook for 20 to 30 seconds more. (Cross your fingers for that puff, but no biggie if you don't get it.)

Transfer the tortilla to a clean kitchen towel and wrap to steam slightly. Then one by one, press and cook the rest. Serve warm.

MASA EN LA CHINGA

- 2 cups masa harina, preferably heirloom corn, plus more as needed
- 2 teaspoons Morton kosher salt
- 2 cups warm water (about 100°F), plus more as needed

Makes 3½ cups

In a medium bowl, combine the masa harina and salt, then pour in the warm water. Use your hands to bring the mixture together into dough, making sure no masa harina stuck to the sides. Knead until no dry patches remain. The dough should feel moist but not sticky, almost like Play-Doh, leaving a light film of residual moisture on your hands. If it's sticky, gradually mix in more masa harina, 1 tablespoon at a time. If it's dry, gradually mix in 1 tablespoon warm water at a time. (Keeps wrapped in plastic in the fridge for up to 2 days.)

BUYING TORTILLAS

Honestly, most of y'all are going to skip the masa and just buy tortillas. That's great, too. Get the best ones you can, preferably freshly pressed from masa (many neighborhood molinos also sell tortillas) or packaged tortillas made without gums or preservatives. The ingredient list should be nothing more than corn, slaked lime, and water. If it's the good stuff, you can pretty much guarantee the shop or label will shout out the word "nixtamalization" somewhere on the sign or label.

If you can't get tortillas made from nixtamalized corn, take a deep breath. We will get through this. You're going to just buy whatever tortillas you can, and it's going to be fine. If you haven't yet tried one made from real masa, however, do that stat. Once you've had that good-good, it's hard to go back.

WARMING TORTILLAS—AND KEEPING THEM WARM . . .

Whether you've made or bought tortillas, you'll probably have to heat them up before you serve them. And unless you're shoving them directly into your mouth, you've got to keep them warm. Here's how.

1) Find you a container that holds in heat. Traditionally in Mexico, that's a woven basket (pretty but not super effective) or a plastic situation (more effective but plastic). You can also get creative with a Dutch oven, insulated lunch bag, or the ultimate: a Yeti cooler. Line it with a kitchen towel.*

2) Get a dry cast-iron skillet, flat griddle, or comal going over medium-high to high heat for a couple minutes. When it's hot enough, you'll notice that when you add the tortillas, they'll give off steam from the undersides. If they don't, just add water.**

3) Work in batches. Add some tortillas in a single layer and cook for 30 to 40 seconds, flipping each one every 10 seconds or so.

4) Transfer those tortillas ASAP into the towel or towel-lined container, wrap them in the towel, then close the container. The heat inside keeps them warm, and the steam keeps them from drying out.

TAQUERO TRICK: When you buy tortillas, you'll typically reheat them on a dry comal or skillet. But sometimes when you eat a taco and the tortilla is really fire, the reason is fat. If you've ever ordered from a taco spot that cooks meat in a choricera, a pot that features a raised platform with a moat around it, you may have noticed the taquero giving the tortillas a lil' dunk in the meat's bubbling fatty juices. Not only does it add flavor, it also helps the tortillas stay hot and soft. It's a vibe thing—you don't always want the addition of fat. But when you do, look to anything from vegetable oil to butter to the fat left over from duck carnitas (see page 225), adding a slick to each side of premade tortillas before reheating them. A little goes a long way.

* My mom skips the container and just uses a thick kitchen towel. That works just fine.

** When you're cooking tortillas, moisture is critical. Our masa has just the right amount, but if yours doesn't or especially if you're buying tortillas, try this. Before your tortillas hit the griddle, give them a lil' misting of water on both sides. Use a spray bottle or just rub a little on. When they hit the griddle, you'll notice a little steam emanating from the bottom. That's good. It'll give you tortillas with a lighter texture. And when you stack them after cooking, they'll be steamier and tastier.

SIN MAÍZ, NO HAY PAÍS

Or in English, "Without corn, there is no country." This was the rallying cry of Mexican activists in the early 2000s. Native corn, the kind that had sustained countless generations, was headed toward extinction. It started with NAFTA. When the trade agreement took effect in 1994, GMO corn from the United States flooded into Mexico, driving down prices. Eventually, many farmers surrendered to the sultry sounds of cheap, high-yielding, pest-resistant monoculture. It was a knife to the heart of finicky, fabulous native corn.

This all coincided with the rise of Maseca, the major brand of instant masa. More and more people chose (with the government's urging) the empty, bland convenience of the shelf-stable powder over the nourishing, flavorful undertaking of proper nixtamalization. Just like coffee went the way of Sanka and bread went Wonder, tortillas became a shell of their former selves.

Yet in the past couple decades, and now more than ever, maíz criollo (or heirloom corn) has shown signs of resurgence. Activists' small legislative victories have yielded support and protections for farmers growing native corn. Mexicans are embracing the old ways of tortilla making as a form of civic action and pride. Molinos and chefs in the US, including us at Nixta, are importing heirloom corn from Mexico, working directly with farmers who are taking on the inconvenient, weighty task. Making and eating good tortillas might be an act of happy indulgence, but it's also an act of politics. Sin maíz, no hay país.

TOSTADAS

Oven-Crunchified Tortillas

We love frying chips, but we love baking tostadas. Low heat purges the moisture from already cooked tortillas, leaving them chip-crisp and nice and light. Just as day-old bread is best for making French toast and croutons, yesterday's tortillas are ideal for tostadas.

Tortillas, as many as you want

Makes as many as you want

Preheat the oven to 325°F.

Bake the tortillas in a single layer directly on the oven rack (or on a wire rack set in a sheet pan), flipping once, until completely crunchy, 20 to 25 minutes. Let them cool completely. (Keeps in an airtight container at room temp for up to 1 week.)

HUEVOS RANCHEROS

Mexi-Brekkie Tostada 'n' Eggs

When Mom made this banger for breakfast, she had me quoting Ice Cube. As I took down sunny-side-ups perched on bean-slathered, slightly crispy tortillas and doused with salsa, all I could think was: Today was a good day. Mama, I just couldn't decide on which salsa of yours I loved more, so I gave the people both.

SALSA ROJA

- 1¾ pounds Roma or plum tomatoes (5 or 6)
- 6 garlic cloves, halved
- 2 small serrano chiles, halved lengthwise
- 1 medium white onion, roughly chopped
- ¾ cup water
- 1 tablespoon chopped epazote or ½ teaspoon dried
- 1½ teaspoons Morton kosher salt, plus more to taste

SALSA VERDE

- 1¼ pounds tomatillos (10 to 14), husked and rinsed
- 6 garlic cloves, halved
- 2 small serrano chiles, halved
- 1 medium white onion, roughly chopped
- ¾ cup water
- ½ cup chopped cilantro
- 1 tablespoon chopped epazote or ½ teaspoon dried
- 1½ teaspoons Morton kosher salt, plus more to taste

HUEVOS RANCHEROS

- 1½ cups Duck-Fat Refried Beans (page 241) or store-bought refrieds
- 12 corn tortillas, preferably day-old
- 2 tablespoons neutral oil, such as grapeseed or canola
- Extra-virgin olive oil, for frying the eggs
- 12 eggs
- Flaky sea salt
- Crumbled queso fresco, for garnish

Serves 4 to 6

MAKE THE SALSA ROJA: In a small pot, combine the tomatoes, garlic, chiles, onion, and water. Bring to a simmer and cook at a gentle simmer, stirring occasionally, until the tomatoes begin to burst, about 25 minutes.

Let cool for 10 minutes. Transfer to a blender, juices and all, add the epazote and salt, then blend until smooth, 1 to 2 minutes. Season to taste with more salt. (Keeps in the fridge for up to 3 days.)

MAKE THE SALSA VERDE: In the same pot or a fresh one while the other cooks, combine the tomatillos, garlic, chiles, onion, and water. Bring to a simmer and cook at a gentle simmer, stirring occasionally, until the tomatillos begin to burst, 20 to 25 minutes.

Let cool for 10 minutes. Transfer to a blender, juices and all, add the cilantro, epazote, and salt and blend until smooth, 1 to 2 minutes. Season to taste with more salt. (Keeps in the fridge for up to 3 days.)

MAKE THE HUEVOS RANCHEROS: If necessary, in a small saucepan, heat the refried beans with a splash of water until hot and spreadable. Warm up the salsas, too.

Line a sheet pan with paper towels and keep it near the stove. Heat a large skillet (preferably nonstick) over medium for a minute or two. Meanwhile, brush or rub the tortillas with the neutral oil. One by one, cook the tortillas, flipping once, until mostly but not totally crunchy, 1 to 2 minutes per side. Drain on the paper towels in a single layer. Spread the refried beans onto one side of the tortillas and transfer to plates.

In the skillet, cook the eggs in batches by heating about 1 tablespoon of olive oil per 2 or 3 eggs over medium-high until it shimmers. Crack the eggs into a bowl, then carefully slide them into the pan. Fry until the whites are set and golden at the edges and the yolks are still runny, 2 to 3 minutes. Top each tortilla with a fried egg and cook the next batch.

Spoon the salsa roja over some and salsa verde over others, leaving the yolks exposed. Season everything with flaky salt, top with the queso fresco, and serve right away.

CHILAQUILES ROJOS

Mexi-Brekkie Chips Smothered in Smoky Salsa

Salsa and chips for breakfast? Yes, please! When this classic morning meal is done right, those chips achieve the glorious middle ground between crunchy and sauce-soaked. Everything else you see here—the beans, the crisp veg, the avocado whizzed with lime—is optional, but highly recommended.

Equipment: deep-fry thermometer

About 6 cups neutral oil, such as grapeseed or canola, for frying
6 corn tortillas, cut into eighths
Kosher salt
2 to 4 eggs
1½ cups Salsa Morita (page 90)

FOR SERVING

1 cup Duck-Fat Refried Beans (page 241) or store-bought refrieds, warmed
Thinly sliced white onion, soaked in ice water a few minutes and then drained
Thinly sliced watermelon radishes
Chopped cilantro
Crumbled queso fresco
Sliced Hass avocado or Avocado Crema (page 89)
Mexican crema
Lime wedges

Serves 2

Set a wire rack or paper towels on a large sheet pan and keep them near the stove. Pour 1½ inches of oil into a large pot or Dutch oven, set over high heat, and bring to 350°F.

Working in 2 batches, fry the tortilla wedges, stirring them for the first few seconds so they don't stick together and flipping them over occasionally, until crispy, about 2 minutes. Use a spider strainer to transfer the chips to the wire rack and sprinkle right away with salt.

Pour out all but ⅛ inch or so of the oil (strain and keep it for future frying adventures). Heat it over medium-high until it shimmers. Crack in the eggs and fry for 2 to 3 minutes, until the whites are set and slightly crispy at the edges and the yolks are still soft and runny. Transfer them to a plate.

Right before serving, pour out all but a tablespoon of the oil, increase the heat to high, and let it smoke lightly. Add the salsa (all at once, to minimize splatter), stir well, then turn off the heat. Add the chips and toss to coat them well in the salsa.

TO SERVE: If necessary, in a small saucepan, heat the refried beans with a splash of water until hot and spreadable. Spread the beans on a serving platter or plates. Add the salsa-fied chips, then top with the onion, radishes, cilantro, queso fresco, avocado, Mexican crema, and finally the fried eggs. Serve with lime wedges.

CHICHARRÓNES EN SALSA VERDE

Pork Rinds 'n' Green Chile Stew

This is my favorite guiso, cozy and chock-full of chicharrónes. You take crispy fried pork skin (easily purchased from a Mexican butcher shop) and simmer it in salsa verde until the chicharrónes slurp it up like a pork sponge and it gets deliciously sogged out. The cooked-stone-fruit acidity of boiled tomatillos and sharp tingle of jalapeños balance the fat, creating a bright, rich stew that's impossible not to tuck into warm tortillas.

- 2½ pounds tomatillos (20 to 24), husked
- 6 jalapeño chiles, stemmed but whole
- 2 serrano chiles, stemmed but whole
- 6 garlic cloves, peeled but whole
- 2 medium white onion, roughly chopped
- 1 bunch of cilantro (stems, too), roughly chopped
- 2 tablespoons granulated chicken bouillon (preferably Knorr)
- 2 tablespoons lard or vegetable oil
- 1¼ pounds chicharrónes (see Note), cut or broken into 1-inch pieces
- Kosher salt

FOR SERVING

- Lots of corn tortillas
- Duck-Fat Refried Beans (optional, but don't play yourself; page 241)

Serves 4

In a medium saucepan, combine the tomatillos, chiles, and enough water to cover by ¼ inch or so (the tomatillos and chiles float, and that's fine). Bring to a nice simmer and cook until the tomatillos turn olive green and are soft but still more or less intact, about 10 minutes.

Use a slotted spoon to transfer the tomatillos and chiles to a blender. Measure out ½ cup of the cooking water in the pan and add to the blender. Add the garlic, onion, cilantro, and granulated bouillon and set aside for 10 minutes or so to cool. Blending super-hot stuff can be dangerous.

Working in 2 batches, blend (if you can, starting on low and gradually increasing to high) until pretty smooth (flecks of cilantro and specks of garlic are just fine), about 1 minute. (Keeps in the fridge for up to 3 days.)

Heat a large skillet set over medium-high. Add the lard and wait until you see wisps of smoke. Quickly and carefully pour in the salsa—quickly to minimize splatter but carefully because some is inevitable. Stirring frequently, let it come to a boil, then reduce to a moderate simmer.

Stir in the chicharrónes, partially cover, and simmer, stirring frequently, until the chicharrónes are tender with a little chew, 20 to 30 minutes. Season to taste with salt.

TO SERVE: While the chicharrónes are simmering, warm and hold the tortillas (see how on page 38).

Serve hot with the beans and tortillas.

NOTE: For this recipe, you want to buy "chicharrónes con carne"—the glorious slabs of puffed skin that have a little meat attached. I love the way those fried meaty bits stay chewy while the skin gets tender. You'll find them at many Mexican and other Latin butcher shops. If you must, buy regular chicharrónes or even bagged pork rinds. It'll still taste great.

ENTOMATADAS

Enchiladas' Cousin—Folded 'n' Covered in Tomato Salsa

A super-homey variation on enchiladas, this Rico family classic features a simple salsa jazzed up with fresh green chiles and granulated bouillon (that's Mexican mom shit right there). Tortillas get dunked in salsa, then folded around queso fresco (Mama Rico might tuck some shredded chicken in there, too). A sprinkle of Cotija, sharp onion, and fresh cilantro, and boom, that's breakfast or light dinner.

SALSA

- 3 pounds Roma or plum tomatoes, cored and cut into 2-inch chunks
- ½ cup chopped yellow onion
- 2 medium serrano chiles, stemmed but whole
- 1 medium jalapeño chile, stemmed but whole
- 2 large garlic cloves, peeled
- 1½ teaspoons granulated tomato bouillon, such as Knorr, or 1 cube
- 1 teaspoon Morton kosher salt, plus more to taste
- 1 cup water
- 1 tablespoon lard (rendered pork fat) or neutral oil

ENTOMATADAS

- About ½ cup neutral oil, such as grapeseed or canola
- 12 corn tortillas
- 1½ cups crumbled queso fresco (6 ounces)
- Finely grated Cotija cheese, for serving
- Thinly sliced yellow onion, for serving
- Finely chopped cilantro, for serving

Serves 4

MAKE THE SALSA: In a medium Dutch oven, combine the tomatoes, onion, chiles, garlic, granulated tomato bouillon, salt, and ½ cup of the water and stir well. Bring to a boil and then lower the heat to cook at a moderate simmer, stirring occasionally, until the tomatoes and chiles are tender, 15 to 20 minutes.

Turn off the heat and let cool a bit. Then transfer to a blender and blend until smooth, about 1 minute.

Heat the lard in a large skillet over medium until it melts and smokes lightly. Add the tomato mixture (watch out for splatter, tomato heads!) and the remaining ½ cup water. Bring to a gentle simmer and cook, stirring occasionally, until thick enough to coat the back of a spoon, 15 to 20 minutes. Season to taste with salt. Remove from the heat and cover to keep warm. (Keeps in the fridge for up to 2 days. Rewarm before using.)

MAKE THE ENTOMATADAS: Pour ¼ inch of oil into a small skillet and heat over medium until it shimmers.

One by one, cook the tortillas for 10 seconds, just until hot and pliable. Transfer to a cutting board, dab with paper towels, and use tongs to submerge them in the salsa and transfer to a shallow serving bowl. Do this for 3 tortillas.

Sprinkle 2 tablespoons of the queso fresco onto each saucy tortilla and fold them in half. Ladle on lots of the remaining salsa, and garnish with the Cotija, sliced onions, and cilantro. Serve right away while you start the next batch.

ENFRIJOLADAS

Enchiladas' Other Cousin—Folded 'n' Covered in Bean Sauce

A staple in Mexican households the world over, homey enfrijoladas are both endlessly comforting and customizable. At their heart, they're tortillas briefly fried, dunked in bean sauce, then folded around something tasty and topped with other things that are tasty. For ours, we dunk in a silky, saucier version of our duck-fat refried beans, fold them around chorizo, and top it with crema and queso fresco. But it's hard to go wrong.

BEAN SAUCE

- 2 tablespoons neutral oil, such as grapeseed or canola
- ½ medium white onion, chopped
- 2 garlic cloves, smashed and peeled
- 1 serrano chile, roughly chopped
- 3 cups Duck-Fat Refried Beans (page 241)
- 1½ cups bean cooking liquid (reserved from the refried beans) or water, plus more as needed
- 1½ teaspoons Morton kosher salt, plus more to taste
- 1 teaspoon dried Mexican oregano

ENFRIJOLADAS

- 10 ounces fresh Mexican chorizo, casings removed
- About ½ cup neutral oil, such as grapeseed or canola, for frying
- 8 corn tortillas
- ½ cup Mexican crema or sour cream
- ½ cup crumbled queso fresco
- 1 large Hass avocado
- ¼ cup thinly sliced red onion
- Chopped cilantro, for sprinkling

Serves 4

MAKE THE BEAN SAUCE: Heat the oil in a medium saucepan over medium until it shimmers. Add the onion, garlic, and chile and cook, stirring, until soft and fragrant, 5 to 7 minutes.

Stir in the beans, bean liquid, salt, and oregano and bring to a simmer. Lower the heat to cook at a gentle simmer, stirring, until slightly thickened, about 10 minutes.

Transfer to a blender and puree until completely smooth, 1 to 2 minutes, gradually adding more bean liquid if necessary. You're after a silky sauce that's just thick enough to coat a spoon. Season with salt, return to the pot, and cover to keep warm.

MAKE THE ENFRIJOLADAS: Cook the chorizo on a dry medium skillet over medium heat, stirring and breaking up clumps, until fully cooked and browned in spots, 7 to 10 minutes. Transfer to a bowl, leaving that magical fat in the skillet, and cover to keep warm.

Pour ¼ inch of oil into the skillet and heat over medium until it shimmers. For one serving, cook 2 tortillas, one at a time, for 10 seconds, just until hot and pliable. Transfer to a cutting board, dab with paper towels, and use tongs to briefly submerge the tortillas in the bean business to coat fully.

Transfer to a serving plate, add some chorizo (like, 3 tablespoons), and fold in half. Lavishly spoon on more bean biz to completely cover the tortillas, drizzle with crema, and sprinkle with queso fresco.

Pit and peel the avocado, then cut into long thin slices. Top with some of the avocado, red onion, and cilantro. Serve right away while you start the next batch.

Repeat with the remaining tortillas, bean biz, and toppings to make 3 more servings.

SIKIL PAK

Mayan Pumpkin Seed 'n' Tomato Dip

We were in the Yucatán, at one of the oldest bars in Mexico, when we saw that a man was surreptitiously scooping a thick paste from a painter's bucket onto our snack plates. Thankfully, we survived and even more thankfully, he had been scooping the fiery dip called sikil pak. In the Mayan language, which is still spoken throughout this Mexican state, sikil means "pumpkin seed" and pak means "tomato," and there's not that much more to it. But toast, roast, and puree it, and the humble mixture becomes seriously and complexly delicious.

Serve it with chips and/or a choose-your-own-adventure crudités, like cucumbers, carrots, and radish—anything crispy or crunchy.

- 1 cup raw hulled pumpkin seeds (pepitas)
- 2 garlic cloves, peeled but whole
- 1 habanero chile, stemmed but whole
- 1 Roma or plum tomato
- ½ medium yellow onion, halved through the root end
- 2 tablespoons extra-virgin olive oil
- 2¼ teaspoons Morton kosher salt, plus more to taste
- 3½ tablespoons freshly squeezed orange juice (from 1 navel orange)
- 1 tablespoon fresh lime juice
- Puffed Amaranth (optional; page 240), for garnish

Serves 4 to 6 as a dip

Toast the pumpkin seeds in a large skillet over medium-high heat, stirring almost constantly, until browned and slightly charred, 5 to 6 minutes. Set aside on a plate.

Preheat the broiler with a rack 3 to 4 inches from heat. Put the garlic, habanero, tomato, and onion on a small sheet pan with some space between them and broil, flipping once or twice, until softened and well charred, 6 to 7 minutes for the garlic and habanero and 15 to 20 minutes for the rest. As they're done, transfer to the blender. Let cool slightly.

To the blender, add the pumpkin seeds, olive oil, salt, orange juice, and lime juice. Blend on high until thick and smooth, like nut butter, 2 to 3 minutes. Season to taste with salt. (Keeps in the fridge for up to 1 week.)

Serve at room temp, sprinkled with the puffed amaranth, if desired, and next to the crispy/crunchy stuff.

AGUACHILE NEGRO

Ceviche's Spicier Cousin

Aguachiles were born in Sinaloa, a state on the west coast of Mexico, but nowadays you can find the dish in half the Mexican restaurants on planet earth. That's because it's so damn good—seafood, often raw and typically shrimp, wading in a soupy, fiery sauce (that's the "aguachile" or chile water). There are green aguachiles, red aguachiles, and then there are aguachiles like this one. The sauce is closer to black (negro) from deep-dark dried chiles and soy sauce, the latter likely the influence of Chinese immigrants to Sinaloa in the nineteenth century.

Shrimp is great, but we love it with scallops, marinated just long enough to soak up those bold, spicy, salty, tart flavors without turning rubbery. A little avocado and cucumber cool things off and tostadas deliver contrasting crunch. Ice-cold beers on the side complete the beach vibes.

SAUCE

- 10 dried chiles de árbol, stemmed (seeded if you scared)
- 2 dried pasilla chiles, stemmed, slit open, and seeded
- 2 dried ancho chiles, stemmed, slit open, and seeded
- ¼ cup black sesame seeds
- 4 garlic cloves, peeled but whole
- 1 cup fresh lime juice (8 to 10 limes)
- ¼ cup tamari or soy sauce
- 2 tablespoons apple cider vinegar
- 1 teaspoon Morton kosher salt, plus more to taste

AGUACHILE

- 1 pound bay scallops
- 1 Hass avocado
- 2 Persian (mini) cucumbers, cut into thin rounds
- ½ cup very thinly sliced red onion
- Flaky sea salt, for serving
- Chopped cilantro, for serving
- Toasted black sesame seeds, for serving
- Tostadas, store-bought or homemade (see page 39), for serving
- Lime wedges, for squeezing

Serves 4 to 6

MAKE THE SAUCE: Heat a dry large skillet over medium-high. Working in batches, add the chiles and toast, shaking the pan and flipping the chiles occasionally, until fragrant and lightly charred, 3 to 4 minutes. When you add the last batch, toss in the sesame seeds so they get toasty, too. Transfer to a blender. Add the garlic to the skillet and cook, flipping occasionally, until charred on all sides, about 8 minutes. Transfer to the blender.

Add the lime juice, tamari, vinegar, and salt to the blender and blend until smooth, 1 to 2 minutes, gradually adding water if necessary. Season to taste with salt.

ASSEMBLE THE DISH: In a shallow serving bowl, toss the bay scallops with about half of the sauce and marinate in the fridge for 15 minutes.

Pour on the remaining sauce. Pit and peel the avocado, then cut into cubes. Nestle in the avocado, cucumbers, and red onion, or do like we do in the photo. Sprinkle on the sea salt, cilantro, and sesame seeds.

Serve with tostadas and lime wedges.

NOTE: I prefer bay scallops here because of their sweetness, but go ahead and dice up some regular scallops, if that's what you've got.

HOT SAUCE

TORTAS DE MILANESA

Big Boy Chicken Cutlet Sandwich

We all love tacos, tamales, and tostadas, but do not sleep on tortas, the monumental Mexican sandwich. They can be filled with almost anything (from hot dogs to eggs to chilaquiles to tamales), but to me, torta de milanesa is king. That's breaded and fried chicken that people way back when associated with Milan, Italy, hence the name. There's nothing like that one-two punch of chewy roll—if you can, hit up a Mexican bakery for bolillos or teleras—and crispy, crunchy filling. Pick and choose the toppings, or even better, use 'em all.

MILANESA

½ cup all-purpose flour
2 eggs
1 tablespoon whole milk
1 cup panko bread crumbs
½ cup fine dried bread crumbs (or pulsed panko)
1 teaspoon ancho chile powder
4 boneless, skinless chicken thighs
1½ teaspoons Morton kosher salt, plus more for sprinkling
Freshly ground black pepper
Neutral oil, such as grapeseed or canola, for shallow-frying

TORTAS

1 cup Duck-Fat Refried Beans (page 241) or store-bought refrieds
4 rolls, preferably bolillos or teleras, split
2 cups finely shredded iceberg lettuce
1 large tomato, sliced ¼ inch thick
2 large Hass avocados
Hot sauce, store-bought or homemade (see page 239)
Avocado Salsa (page 89)
¾ cup Pickled Red Onions (page 93)
½ cup crumbled queso fresco

Serves 4

MAKE THE MILANESA: Set up a dredging station with three shallow dishes: In one shallow dish, dump the flour. In a second dish, beat the eggs with the milk. In a third, stir together the panko bread crumbs, fine bread crumbs, and ancho powder.

One at a time, sandwich the chicken thighs between pieces of plastic wrap and pound with the back of a small heavy skillet so they're evenly ½ inch thick. Season all over with the salt and pepper to taste.

Coat the thighs in the flour, shaking off any excess, then coat them in the egg mixture, then in the bread crumbs, turning and patting. Let them sit on a plate for 15 minutes for extra crispiness.

Set a wire rack in a sheet pan and keep them near the stove. Pour ½ inch oil into a large skillet and heat over medium-high. To tell when it's hot enough, dip in a wooden chopstick or handle of a wooden spoon. When you immediately see little bubbles, we good.

Working in batches to avoid overcrowding, fry the thighs until golden brown and crispy, flipping once, 4 to 5 minutes total. Transfer to the rack and immediately sprinkle lightly with salt.

MAKE THE TORTAS: If necessary, in a small saucepan, heat the refried beans with a splash of water until hot and spreadable. Keep warm.

On a hot dry cast-iron skillet or griddle over medium heat, toast the rolls cut-sides down until lightly golden, 1 to 2 minutes. (If you're not using bolillos or teleras, consider swiping a little butter on them first.)

Spread the beans on the bottom halves of each roll. Add the lettuce, tomato, and chicken. Pit and peel the avocados, then cut them into long thin slices. Top with sliced avocado, hot sauce, avocado salsa, pickled onions, and finally, queso fresco. Close them up, give them a light press, and eat!

HUARACHES DE NOPALES

Masa "Sandals" with Cactus

These oblong disks of masa truly are about the size and shape of my tía Mona's flip-flops (in Spanish, *huarache* means sandal). They can be topped with virtually anything—from pickled pig skin to grilled steak—yet one of my favorites is nopales. If you've never had them, cactus paddles, which are typically sold despined at Mexican markets, have a touch of tartness and an ever-so-slightly-juicy snap, clocking in somewhere between green bean and okra. An easy-peasy pico de gallo made with sweet cherry tomatoes delivers a wallop of salt, acid, and heat.

NOPALES

- 1 tablespoon neutral oil, such as grapeseed or canola
- 1 pound trimmed nopales (cactus paddles), cut into ¼-inch dice
- 2 garlic cloves, minced
- 1 teaspoon Morton kosher salt, plus more to taste
- 2 tablespoons salsa macha, store-bought or homemade (see page 91)

HUARACHES

- 2 cups fresh masa or Masa en la Chinga (page 37)
- Cherry Tomato Pico de Gallo (page 92)
- Chopped cilantro, for serving
- Big chunk of queso fresco, for serving
- Lime wedges, for serving

Serves 4

COOK THE NOPALES: Heat the oil in a large skillet over medium until it shimmers. Add the nopales, garlic, and salt and cook, stirring, until the liquid that comes out after a few minutes has evaporated, 8 to 10 minutes. Turn off the heat. Stir in the salsa macha, season to taste with salt, and keep warm until serving.

MAKE THE HUARACHES: Heat a large dry cast-iron skillet or griddle over medium until nice and hot. You're going to form one huarache at a time and transfer it straight to the hot skillet.

Prepare two 9-inch squares of parchment paper or plastic wrap. Divide the masa into 4 equal portions. Working with one at a time, roll a portion into a 3-inch-long torpedo shape. Put the masa torpedo on the parchment paper, cover with the other piece, and either roll with a rolling pin or gently press with the bottom of a skillet to make an oval about 8 inches long and ¼ inch thick (huaraches, baby!).

Transfer it straight to the skillet, then repeat to add as many more huaraches as can comfortably fit in the pan. Cook the huaraches, flipping once, until cooked through, 3 minutes per side. Transfer to a platter or plates as they're done.

Divide the nopales among the huaraches, then add a spoonful of pico, leaving most of the juices behind. Garnish with cilantro, use a Microplane to generously grate on the queso fresco, and serve with lime wedges on the side.

TACOS DE PULPO

Tentacle Tacos

Octopus tacos sound wild—unless you've been to Mexico. Then you know that just about every sea creature makes it onto tortillas, from the crab tostadas in Mexico City to the lobster burritos in Baja.

Each component of this dish plays a crucial role, so follow my lead. There's the tortilla, slightly charred and crisp, yet not quite a tostada. There's a swipe of refried beans for creamy depth. There's the octopus, simmered until tender (which is so much easier than cephalopod newbies might expect) and then seared in a skillet. On the plate, there's aguachile—a blend of little more than lime juice, serrano chiles, and cilantro that's bright and fiery. Coastal vibes, big flavor, thrilling party food.

OCTOPUS

- 4 garlic cloves, smashed and peeled
- 1 medium white onion, halved
- 1 bay leaf
- 6 tablespoons Morton kosher salt
- 1 whole octopus (1½ to 2 pounds), cleaned

AGUACHILE

- 1½ cups fresh lime juice (12 to 16 limes)
- ¼ cup chopped cilantro
- 2 tablespoons extra-virgin olive oil
- 1 teaspoon Morton kosher salt
- 2 serrano chiles (seeded if you scared), roughly chopped
- 1 garlic clove, peeled but whole

TACOS

- ½ cup Duck-Fat Refried Beans (page 241) or store-bought refrieds
- 8 corn tortillas
- Neutral oil, such as grapeseed or canola
- Kosher salt
- 1 Hass avocado
- ½ cup Pickled Red Onions (page 93)
- Little cilantro sprigs
- Lime wedges, for squeezing

Makes 8 tacos

COOK THE OCTOPUS: In a large pot, combine the garlic, onion, bay leaf, salt, and 10 cups water and bring to a boil. Holding the octopus by the head with tongs, dip the tentacles in and out of the water until they curl, 2 or 3 times.

Next, add the octopus to the pot, return to a simmer, and adjust the heat to simmer gently until a small sharp knife can pierce the legs as if they were softened butter, 30 to 45 minutes.

Remove the octopus (discard the cooking liquid and solids) and let the octopus cool slightly. Cut the individual tentacles from the octopus. The goal here is one tentacle per taco, but you should definitely use the head, too. Remove and discard the beak, chop up the head, and sear it for extra tacos. (Keeps in the fridge for up to 2 days.)

MEANWHILE, MAKE THE AGUACHILE: In a blender, combine the lime juice, cilantro, oil, salt, chiles, and garlic. Blend until smooth, 1 to 2 minutes. Refrigerate until ready to serve, up to 1 day.

MAKE THE TACOS: If necessary, in a small saucepan, heat the refried beans with a splash of water until hot and spreadable. Keep warm.

Preheat the oven to 350°F. Line a tray with paper towels and keep them near the oven.

Generously rub one side of each tortilla with oil and season lightly with salt. Arrange them oil-side down on a large sheet pan and bake until the bottoms are deep golden brown and slightly crispy but the tortillas are still foldable, 6 to 8 minutes. Transfer browned-side down to the paper towels to drain briefly.

Meanwhile, heat a large heavy skillet over medium-high. Add 2 tablespoons oil and let it smoke lightly. Pat the octopus tentacles dry, then working in batches, cook the tentacles until golden and crisp on both sides, flipping once, 6 to 8 minutes total. Season with salt and set aside.

Divide the aguachile among four serving plates. Pit and peel the avocado, then cut into 8 long thin slices.

Spoon a layer of beans onto the unbrowned side of each tortilla, add a tentacle and avocado slice, and top with pickled onions and cilantro sprigs. Set them on the aguachile and serve right away with lime wedges.

TACOS DE PESCADO (ESTILO ENSENADA)

Perfectly Crunchy 'n' Airy Fish Tacos

I grew up within striking distance of Baja California (that's a state in Mexico, y'all), so I've known fish tacos could be fire. But it wasn't until Sara and I took a trip down to Ensenada, a port city there, that I realized they belong in the upper taco echelon alongside attention-hogging greats like barbacoa and carnitas.

At a stand called Tacos Fenix, we marveled at three señoras who ran the place with Navy SEAL–like precision, battering and frying fish in a pot of lard to absolute perfection. Those inspired these, which are extra light and crisp thanks to masa harina in the typical all-flour batter. And to ice-cold vodka, the advice of friend and fish-and-chips legend Ed Szymanski. Sometimes we get wild and drizzle on a little Salsa Macha (page 91) or even Chinese chili crisp.

Equipment: deep-fry thermometer

CHIPOTLE CREMA

½ cup Mexican crema or sour cream
1 canned chipotle chile in adobo sauce, finely minced
1 tablespoon adobo sauce (from the can)
1 teaspoon fresh lime juice, plus more to taste
½ teaspoon Morton kosher salt

FISH

1½ pounds skinless halibut fillets (grouper or mahi mahi work great, too)
Morton kosher salt and freshly ground black pepper
Neutral oil, such as grapeseed or canola, for deep-frying
⅔ cup masa harina, preferably heirloom corn
10½ tablespoons cornstarch, plus more as needed
1 egg white
½ cup plus 1 tablespoon sparkling water, very cold
½ cup ice-cold vodka

TACOS

10 corn tortillas
2 cups packed very finely shredded red cabbage
Pico de Gallo (page 92) or Salsa de Habanero (page 92)
Lime wedges, for squeezing

Makes 8 tacos

MAKE THE CHIPOTLE CREMA: In a small bowl, whisk together the crema, chipotle, adobo sauce, lime juice, and salt. Season to taste with lime and salt and refrigerate until ready to use.

PREP AND COOK THE FISH: Stick a medium mixing bowl in the freezer for at least 15 minutes. Cut the fish into 8 strips that are about 1 inch wide and 4 to 5 inches long. Lightly season the fish all over with salt and pepper.

Set a wire rack in a sheet pan and keep them near the stove. Pour 3 inches oil into a large pot and heat over high to 350°F.

Meanwhile, into a small mixing bowl, sift the masa harina, cornstarch, and ½ teaspoon salt and mixy mixy. Set aside. In another small mixing bowl, whisk the egg whites vigorously until bubbly and roughly doubled in volume, 30 seconds to 1 minute. Set aside.

Take out the frozen bowl, add the sparkling water and vodka, and mixy mixy. About a tablespoon at a time, add the masa harina mixture to the liquid mixture, whisking to incorporate so no dry spots remain. Add the eggs and mix until smooth. If necessary, gradually add more cornstarch so the mixture is a little thicker than pancake batter. If I were you, I'd add the bowl to another bowl of very icy water to keep it extra cold.

When the oil is ready, fry the fish in two batches like so: One at a time, submerge the fish pieces in the batter, let any excess drip off, then add them to the oil.

Fry, moving them around occasionally, until golden and puffed, 2 to 3 minutes. As they're fried, transfer to the wire rack and immediately season lightly with salt. Let the oil return to temp before frying the next batch.

ASSEMBLE THE TACOS: Warm and hold the tortillas (see how on page 38).

Serve the fish hot with warm tortillas. Top with the cabbage, chipotle crema, and pico de gallo. Serve with lime wedges.

TACOS DE RAJAS CON CREMA

Creamy, Cheesy Roasted Poblano Tacos

Right before we officially opened Nixta, I had the absolute pleasure of cooking for my extended family, flown in fresh from California and filling up the tables in our 600-square-foot dining room. By my side in the kitchen were the women who taught me to cook, helping me make this Mexican classic. Abuelita was roasting and peeling poblanos like a boss. Mom was chopping onions faster than any culinary school grad. All was well until I busted out the Gruyère.

Eyebrows shot up. Crucifixes were clutched. Yet the matriarchs relented and let me work my magic. That night, they were there to help cook *my* food, after all. Gruyère added a touch of funk and Ecuadorian crema contributed its particular tang, both ingredients as foreign to my fam as an alien invasion. I hauled the creamy, tangy, smoky, sweet result to the table and ultimately received the only seal of approval that matters. Not a bite was left.

RAJAS CON CREMA

- 1½ pounds poblano chiles (about 5 medium)
- 2 ears corn, husks on
- ¼ cup neutral oil, such as grapeseed or canola
- 2 garlic cloves, finely chopped
- 1 medium white onion, finely chopped
- 1 cup crema, preferably Ecuadorian
- 1 cup whole milk
- ¼ cup heavy cream
- ½ cup shredded Monterey Jack cheese
- ¼ cup shredded Gruyère cheese
- ¼ cup shredded extra-sharp white cheddar cheese
- 1 tablespoon Morton kosher salt

TACOS

- 16 to 20 corn tortillas
- Crumbled queso fresco
- Cilantro leaves
- Extra-virgin olive oil, for drizzling
- Flaky sea salt, for sprinkling
- Lime wedges, for squeezing

Makes 16 to 20 tacos

MAKE THE RAJAS CON CREMA: Preheat the oven broiler with a rack 3 to 4 inches from the heat. Put the poblanos on a large sheet pan with some space between them and broil, flipping twice, until blistered and charred all over, 15 to 20 minutes. Transfer those babies to a large bowl, cover tightly, and let them chill out for 20 minutes, until they're cool enough to handle.

Meanwhile, cook the ears of corn directly over a stovetop flame, turning occasionally, until the husks are completely charred, 3 to 5 minutes. (Or cook them shucked under the broiler until lightly charred.)

Let the corn cool for a couple of minutes, then shuck and cut off the kernels, discarding the cobs. When the poblanos have cooled, pull off the stems, scrape off the skins as best you can (no rinsing, though!), then scrape out the seeds and veins and discard them. Cut the flesh into long strips ¼ inch wide.

Heat the oil in a large skillet over medium until it shimmers. Add the garlic and onions and cook, stirring occasionally, until translucent and slightly softened, about 6 minutes.

Stir in the poblanos and corn, then add the crema, milk, and heavy cream and bring to a low simmer. Adjust the heat to simmer gently until the flavors come together and the liquid thickens enough to coat the back of a spoon, about 10 minutes. Sometimes the sauce splits—no biggie!

Turn off the heat, add all three cheeses and the salt, and stir until the cheeses have completely melted. Keep warm off the heat.

ASSEMBLE THE TACOS: Meanwhile, warm and hold the tortillas (see how on page 38).

Serve the rajas with the tortillas, queso fresco, and cilantro. Have everyone make their own tacos finished with a drizzle of olive oil, a sprinkle of flaky sea salt, and a squeeze of lime juice.

TACOS DE CARNE ASADA

Grilled Steak Tacos

My dad used to grill up dope carne asada, steak in the style of Northern Mexico marinated in citrus and beer. When I make carne asada, I apply a few of the culinary nuggets I picked up from my travels. For example, right before the charred meat comes off the grill, I give one side a squeeze of orange juice and a smooch of heat—a taquero trick that takes the flavor to the next level. (Dad did this but with beer.) If you want to be rowdy, serve the steak costra-style, aka on cheesy open-faced tortillas.

On the side, grilled spring onions provide sweetness and charred jalapeños smoky heat.

Equipment: charcoal or gas grill

CARNE ASADA

- ½ cup light Mexican beer, such as Modelo Especial
- ⅓ cup extra-virgin olive oil, plus more for grilling
- ¼ cup fresh lime juice (2 to 3 limes)
- ¼ cup freshly squeezed orange juice (from 1 juicy orange)
- 2 teaspoons dried Mexican oregano
- Kosher salt
- 1 teaspoon freshly ground black pepper
- 1 medium white onion, thinly sliced
- 4 garlic cloves, finely grated
- 2 pounds skirt steak, cut into a few pieces

FOR GRILLING

- Neutral oil, such as grapeseed or canola
- Kosher salt
- 8 jalapeño chiles
- 8 large spring onions (see Note, page 201), roots and any busted tops trimmed
- 1 orange, halved
- 12 corn tortillas
- 1 pound Chihuahua cheese, coarsely shredded

FOR SERVING

- Salsa de Chiltepín (page 91)
- Lime wedges
- Flaky sea salt

Serves 6

MARINATE THE STEAK: In a resealable bag or shallow baking dish, whisk together the beer, olive oil, lime juice, orange juice, oregano, 1 tablespoon salt, and the pepper. Stir in the onion and garlic. Add the skirt steak and turn to coat and get it more or less submerged in the marinade. Marinate at room temperature for at least 2 hours or refrigerate for up to 8 hours, flipping the meat once halfway through.

GET GRILLING: If your steak is marinating in the fridge, take it out an hour or so before you cook it to bring it to room temperature.

Prepare a charcoal or gas grill to cook with high heat. Remove the steak from the marinade, wipe it off, and pat dry. Rub with a little oil and season lightly with salt.

Grill the jalapeños and spring onions, turning occasionally, until charred and tender, 8 to 10 minutes.

Grill the steak on the hottest part of the grill, flipping occasionally, until deeply charred on both sides, 6 to 8 minutes total for medium-rare or medium.

Just before you pull the steak, give the topside a good squeeze of orange juice and flip it to give the juice a little smooch of heat. Transfer to a cutting board to rest for 10 minutes or so.

Meanwhile, stick a skillet or griddle on the grill and let it heat up. In batches, heat the tortillas on the grill (on a moderately hot area, if you can) for 15 to 30 seconds per side. Add the cheese to one side of each tortilla and cook undisturbed until just melted, 1 to 2 minutes. Flip them cheese-side down and let the cheese get a little browned and crusty, about 15 seconds, then use a spatula to dislodge the cheese from the pan and flip them tortilla-side down onto a tray or platter.

TO SERVE: Slice the steak against the grain. Serve with the grilled vegetables, cheesy tortillas, salsa, and lime wedges on the side. Finish with flaky sea salt.

TACOS DE COCHINITA PIBIL

Yucatán-Style Slow-Roasted Pork Tacos

Edgar had planned to propose to me in the Yucatán, but there were too many wild hogs running around. Plus, we were busy eating cochinita pibil—gorgeous hunks of pork that have been rubbed with recado rojo (a mixture of annatto seeds, citrus, and spices), wrapped in banana leaves, and cooked in underground pits called pibs. Now, we can't guarantee that Edgar's oven-friendly version will get you a "yes," but let's just say it didn't *not* help me get there.

MARINATED PORK

- 2 tablespoons lard or vegetable oil
- ⅓ cup finely ground annatto seeds (aka achiote)
- 3 tablespoons dried Mexican oregano
- 2 tablespoons black peppercorns
- 1 tablespoon allspice berries
- 1 tablespoon cumin seeds
- 1 tablespoon coriander seeds
- 5 whole cloves
- One 3-inch cinnamon stick
- ¾ cup orange juice
- ¼ cup fresh lime juice (2 to 3 limes)
- ¼ cup white wine vinegar
- 3 tablespoons Morton kosher salt
- 12 garlic cloves, peeled but whole
- 5½ to 6 pounds bone-in skinless pork shoulder, fat cap left on

FOR BAKING

- One 1-pound package banana leaves (6 to 8), fresh or thawed frozen, wiped with a wet towel
- 1 medium white onion, sliced ¼ inch thick
- 10 bay leaves

TACOS

- Lots of corn tortillas
- Pickled Red Onions (page 93)
- Salsa de Habanero (optional; page 92)

Serves 8 to 10

MARINATE THE PORK: Heat the lard in a medium skillet over medium until shimmering. Add the annatto seeds, oregano, peppercorns, allspice, cumin, coriander, cloves, and cinnamon and stir until aromatic, about 3 minutes. Transfer to a blender along with the orange juice, lime juice, vinegar, salt, and garlic and blend until smooth, 1 to 2 minutes.

Put the pork shoulder in a large container, pour on the marinade, and rub to coat evenly and all over. Cover and refrigerate for 8 to 12 hours.

BAKE THE PORK: Preheat the oven to 275°F.

On a work surface, lay down 4 unbroken banana leaves, shiny-side down and overlapping, to make a bed for the pork. Set the pork in the center and scatter the onion and bay leaves on top. Fold the leaves over and tuck the sides under to make an airtight package.

Transfer the package to a large sheet pan or aluminum baking pan. Top with the remaining banana leaves, tucking them around the package, and transfer to the oven.

Cook in the oven until the meat is so tender that a table knife slides in with zero resistance, about 8 hours.

ASSEMBLE THE TACOS: About 15 minutes before the pork is done, warm and hold the tortillas (see how on page 38).

Remove the pork from the oven and use oven mitts to transfer the package to a large bowl. Carefully unwrap the pork, discarding the banana and bay leaves. Use two forks to shred the hot meat, then toss the pork with its drippings.

Serve hot with warm tortillas, pickled red onions, and salsa.

ENCHILADAS POTOSINAS

Edgar's Hometown Enchiladas

Don't get it twisted. These aren't enchiladas like you've ever had them before, unless your family, like mine, is also from San Luis Potosí. Not only that, they're my riff on the local dish, so even Potosinos might not fully recognize them—until they take a bite. The tortillas here aren't dunked in salsa and rolled, but rather served open-faced and slathered with refried black beans and chorizo-charged potato mash, then topped with shredded cabbage, roasted tomato salsa, and funky aged cheese called queso enchilado (or Parm, if you must).

POTATO-CHORIZO MASH

2 pounds Yukon Gold potatoes (about 6), unpeeled
8 ounces fresh Mexican chorizo, casings removed
2 teaspoons Morton kosher salt

TOMATO SALSA

½ cup neutral oil, such as grapeseed or canola
10 ounces Roma or plum tomatoes, cored and quartered
½ medium yellow onion, quartered
1 small garlic clove, peeled but whole
1½ teaspoons dried Mexican oregano
1 teaspoon Morton kosher salt, plus more to taste

ENCHILADAS POTOSINAS

3 dried guajillo chiles, stemmed, slit open, and seeded
1 cup water
Neutral oil, such as grapeseed or canola
10 corn tortillas
¾ cup Duck-Fat Refried Beans (page 241), warmed
3 cups very thinly sliced red cabbage
⅔ cup finely grated (on a box grater) queso enchilado

Makes 10 enchiladas

NOTE: For the classic, my brethren mix guajillo chiles into the masa to stunt on y'all. Since you're probably buying tortillas to make the dish, the recipe asks you to dunk the tortillas in pureed guajillos to give them that red color and fruity guajillo flavor.

MAKE THE POTATO-CHORIZO MASH: In a medium pot, combine the potatoes with water to cover by 2 inches and bring to a boil. Lower the heat to cook at a steady simmer until a knife goes in with zero pressure but before they start to fall apart, about 30 minutes. Drain and wipe out the pot.

In the same pot, cook the chorizo over medium heat, occasionally breaking up clumps so it's nice and fine, until it's fully cooked but not browned, 7 to 8 minutes. Return the potatoes to the pot, add the salt, then mashy mashy until smoothish. (At this point, you can refrigerate the mash for up to 5 days.)

MAKE THE TOMATO SALSA: Heat the oil in a medium saucepan over medium-high until it shimmers. Add the tomatoes and onion and cook, stirring occasionally, until the tomatoes break down, about 8 minutes, adding the garlic halfway through. Let cool slightly.

Add the oregano and salt and blend with an immersion blender (your best bet) or a regular blender (you'll probably have to stop and stir to help it catch) until completely smooth. Season to taste with salt. (At this point, you can refrigerate the salsa for up to 3 days.)

MAKE THE ENCHILADA POTOSINAS: Heat a large skillet over medium-high for a minute. Add the chiles and toast, flipping frequently, until fragrant and slightly darkened, about 1 minute. In a blender, combine the chiles, water, and 2 tablespoons of oil and blend until smooth. Set aside in a shallow bowl.

Pour ¼ inch of oil into a small skillet and heat over medium until it shimmers. One by one, cook the tortillas for 10 seconds, just until hot and pliable. As they're done, give them a lil' shake to remove any excess oil and stack them to help keep them warm.

Heat the large skillet over medium-high. One by one, dip the tortillas in the guajillo mixture to coat, let the excess drip off, and then cook in batches for 30 seconds per side to give the puree a chance to cook. Transfer to plates.

Now, here's how we do it: To the center of each tortilla, add a tablespoon of the beans and spread them out a bit. Next, add 3 tablespoons of the potato-chorizo mash. Top with the cabbage, drizzle on about 1 tablespoon of the tomato salsa in a zigzag, then sprinkle on the cheese. Serve right away.

EMPANADAS DE BARBACOA

Slow-Cooked Beef Handpie—aka Mexican Sambusa

In Mexico, empanadas can be filled with everything from chicken to tuna, pineapple to cheese. We go with the creative flow, giving succulent beef cheeks the Northern-style barbacoa treatment and then tucking them inside masa pockets. Braised with dried chiles and spices until rich and gelatinous, the cheeks make a fantastic taco topper, too. Either way, smoky salsa is key and the second bright salsa made from pineapple is extra credit.

Also, evidence suggests that empanadas were born in BCE Persia, which itself suggests that Sara's baba is right—Iranians did invent everything.

Equipment: deep-fry thermometer

BARBACOA

- 2 dried pasilla chiles, stemmed, slit open, and seeded
- 1 dried ancho chile, stemmed, slit open, and seeded
- 1 teaspoon cumin seeds
- 1 teaspoon black peppercorns
- 2 tablespoons beef tallow or neutral oil, such as grapeseed or canola
- 3 whole beef cheeks (about 2 pounds) or beef chuck cut into 3 pieces
- Morton kosher salt
- 4 cups unsalted beef stock
- 5 garlic cloves, peeled but whole
- 2 bay leaves
- 1 medium white onion, quartered

EMPANADAS

- 2½ cups fresh masa or Masa en la Chinga (page 37)
- 2 tablespoons beef tallow or pork lard, gently warmed, or neutral oil, such as grapeseed or canola
- ½ teaspoon Morton kosher salt
- 1 tablespoon warm water
- Neutral oil, such as grapeseed or canola, for frying

FOR SERVING

- Salsa Morita (page 90)
- Tepache Salsa (recipe follows)

Makes 10 empanadas (plus extra barbacoa for tacos)

MAKE THE BARBACOA: Heat a dry medium skillet over medium. Add the chiles and toast, flipping the chiles occasionally, until fragrant, about 2 minutes. Soak in hot water for 20 minutes until softened.

Reserving the soaking liquid, scoop out the chiles and transfer to a blender. Add the cumin, peppercorns, and ½ cup of the soaking liquid and blend until smooth, about 2 minutes, gradually adding more of the soaking liquid if necessary.

Heat the tallow in a large Dutch oven over medium-high until hot. Pat the beef dry and generously season all over with salt. Sear the beef until browned on all sides, about 12 minutes total. Add the stock, garlic, bay leaves, onion, 1 tablespoon salt, and the blended chile mixture and bring to a simmer. Cover and cook at a gentle simmer until the meat is shreddably tender, 3 to 3½ hours for cheeks or 2 to 2½ hours for chuck.

Transfer the beef to a bowl and set aside. Crank the heat and let the liquid left in the pot bubble away, stirring occasionally, until reduced by about half, 15 to 20 minutes.

Meanwhile, shred the beef. When the liquid has reduced, strain it into the bowl with the beef, discarding the solids, and toss well. If using to fill the empanadas, let cool, then refrigerate until fully chilled, at least 3 hours or up to 2 days.

CONTINUED

NOTE: Could you skip the beef tallow? Totally. But it's a hard-recommend from us—not only does it double down on the beefy flavor of the filling, it also gives the dough extra crispiness. If you're feeling real rowdy, use tallow for the frying, too.

MAKE THE EMPANADAS: In a large bowl, combine the masa, tallow, and salt and knead to mix well. Add the water and knead until incorporated.

Grab a ball of the masa dough about the size of a golf ball (70 grams, if you're a weigher), sandwich it between two pieces of plastic wrap, and use a tortilla press or the bottom of a glass pie plate to press into an even 5- to 6-inch round. Add 2 tablespoons of the barbacoa to one side of the round, fold over the other side to form a half-moon, gently pressing the edges to seal. Feel free to get freaky and crimp the edges. Repeat with remaining dough and filling. Now, get to frying.

Set a wire rack over a sheet pan and keep them near the stove. Pour 2 inches of oil into a Dutch oven and heat over medium to 350°F. Working in batches to avoid overcrowding, cook the empanadas until golden all over, flipping once, 3 to 4 minutes total. Transfer to the rack to drain and let the oil come back to temp between batches. (Strain and keep the oil for future frying adventures.)

Serve hot with the salsas for dipping.

TEPACHE SALSA

1 cup chopped pineapple (or pineapple flesh, not core, leftover from making the tepache)
½ cup tepache, store-bought or homemade (see page 95)
1 fresh habanero chile, halved
1 tablespoon fresh lime juice
½ teaspoon Morton kosher salt, plus more to taste

Makes about 1¼ cups

In a blender, stir to combine the pineapple, tepache, habanero, lime juice, and salt. Let sit for 10 to 15 minutes to meld the flavors.

Blend on high until smooth, about 2 minutes. Season with salt to taste. (Keeps in the fridge for up to 12 hours.)

MAMA RICO'S CHORIZO MEATLOAF

Mom cooked only Mexican at home until the day I returned from school asking why she didn't know how to make the pizza and nuggets that the other kids were eating. That was the good stuff, I thought. Why must I always be tormented with beans and tortillas?

Soon after, I came home to find her making a classic American dish—meatloaf and mashed potatoes. The potatoes were from a box. The meatloaf recipe was clipped from the newspaper. I thought I was in red, white, and blue nirvana, but looking back, her meatloaf was Mexican through and through. Because like the good cook she was, she didn't follow the recipe to the letter. Instead, she instinctively borrowed from her pantry, incorporating chorizo, chiles, cumin, and cilantro so it vibed with the flavors we liked. They go so well with the potatoes I learned to make at my first steakhouse job.

GLAZE

- ¾ cup ketchup
- 1 tablespoon finely minced canned chipotle chiles in adobo sauce
- 1 tablespoon apple cider vinegar
- 1 teaspoon brown sugar
- 1 teaspoon Morton kosher salt

MEATLOAF

- 1 tablespoon neutral oil
- ¾ cup finely chopped white onion
- 2 garlic cloves, minced
- 1 serrano or small jalapeño chile (seeded if you scared), finely chopped
- 1 pound ground beef, preferably 80/20
- 8 ounces fresh Mexican chorizo, casings removed
- 2 eggs
- ¾ cup panko bread crumbs
- 2 tablespoons whole milk
- 2 teaspoons Worcestershire sauce
- 2 tablespoons thinly sliced cilantro stems
- 1 tablespoon Morton kosher salt
- ½ teaspoon freshly ground black pepper
- ½ teaspoon ground cumin
- ½ teaspoon dried Mexican oregano
- ¼ teaspoon smoked paprika

FOR SERVING

- Scallion Mashed Potatoes (recipe follows)
- Sliced scallions

Serves 4 to 6

MAKE THE GLAZE: In a small bowl, combine the ketchup, chipotle, vinegar, brown sugar, and salt and mixy mixy. Set aside.

MAKE THE MEATLOAF: Preheat the oven to 375°F.

Heat the oil in a small skillet over medium. Add the onion, garlic, and chile, stirring, until soft and fragrant, 4 to 6 minutes. Let cool.

In a large bowl, combine the cooled onion mixture, the beef, chorizo, eggs, panko, milk, Worcestershire sauce, cilantro stems, salt, pepper, cumin, oregano, and smoked paprika. Use your hands to mix just until everything is well distributed.

Lay out three 2-foot pieces of foil, overlapping slightly, to make a square. Transfer the meat mixture to the center of the edge closest to you and pat to make a log 10 inches long. Roll the foil over the meat and keep rolling, patting the top and sides to make a tight, neat-ish cylinder. Roll up the sides to close them and pat to make that log nice and tight.

Put the package seam-side up on a large sheet pan and bake for 35 minutes.

Carefully open the foil to expose the top of the meatloaf, spoon on the chipotle glaze, then spread to an even layer. Return to the oven and bake, uncovered, until the glaze caramelizes slightly and the meatloaf is cooked through (cut in for a sneak peek, or if you're a thermometer person, pull it at 160°F), 20 minutes.

Let it rest for 10 minutes.

TO SERVE: Spoon the scallion mash onto a serving platter. Slice the loaf into rounds 1 inch thick and arrange them on top. Garnish with scallions and serve.

CONTINUED

NOTE: You can totally bake this in a loaf pan, but the foil wrapping not only results in a juicier product, it also gives you cool round slices.

SCALLION MASHED POTATOES

2 pounds Yukon Gold potatoes, peeled and cut into 1-inch dice
3 tablespoons Morton kosher salt, plus more to taste
8 tablespoons (4 ounces/1 stick) unsalted butter, cubed
1 cup heavy cream
¾ cup whole milk
1 bunch of scallions, thinly sliced, whites and greens kept separate

Serves 4 to 6

In a medium pot, combine the potatoes, salt, and enough water to cover by 1 inch. Bring to a simmer and cook at a moderate simmer until creamy-tender but not falling apart, 12 to 15 minutes. Drain well, dump the potatoes back in the pot, and let them steam-dry for a few minutes.

Meanwhile, in a small saucepan, combine the butter, heavy cream, milk, and scallion whites. Set over medium-low heat until steamy, about 12 minutes. Cook over low heat for 4 minutes, to fully infuse with scallion flavor. Remove from the heat.

Mash the potatoes until smooth, then stir in the butter mixture and season with salt to taste. Stir in the scallion greens just before serving.

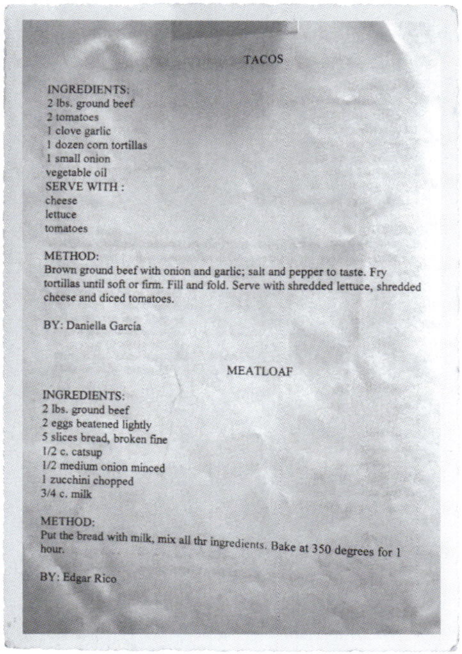

TACOS

INGREDIENTS:
2 lbs. ground beef
2 tomatoes
1 clove garlic
1 dozen corn tortillas
1 small onion
vegetable oil
SERVE WITH :
cheese
lettuce
tomatoes

METHOD:
Brown ground beef with onion and garlic; salt and pepper to taste. Fry tortillas until soft or firm. Fill and fold. Serve with shredded lettuce, shredded cheese and diced tomatoes.

BY: Daniella García

MEATLOAF

INGREDIENTS:
2 lbs. ground beef
2 eggs beatened lightly
5 slices bread, broken fine
1/2 c. catsup
1/2 medium onion minced
1 zucchini chopped
3/4 c. milk

METHOD:
Put the bread with milk, mix all thr ingredients. Bake at 350 degrees for 1 hour.

BY: Edgar Rico

Edgar and Mama Rico at the James Beard Awards when he won that year! She brought along a book of his from elementary school—it's his first "published" recipes! The man loved meatloaf from Day 1.

ENCHILADAS SUIZAS

Rolled 'n' Covered in Green Salsa and Cheese

Suiza means Swiss in Spanish, but these enchiladas are Mexican through and through. My first time eating this gooey, creamy, tangy dish was at a Mexico City Sanborns, a chain of department stores with cafes attached, where legend has it, the dish was invented in the 1950s. Inspired by immigrants to Mexico from Switzerland or just by the notion of the dairy-loving Swiss, the chef at the time tweaked a traditional salsa verde made from tomatillos with cream and topped the enchiladas with cheese. The result was tradition enriched by innovation, cultural intermingling at its finest, something brand-new that became a classic.

SALSA

1 pound medium tomatillos (8 to 12), husked and rinsed
2 jalapeño chiles, stemmed but whole
2 serrano chiles, stemmed but whole
1 bunch of cilantro, bottoms trimmed, roughly chopped
2 garlic cloves, peeled but whole
1¼ cups heavy cream
¼ cup sour cream
1 teaspoon Morton kosher salt, plus more to taste
1 teaspoon granulated chicken bouillon
½ teaspoon freshly ground black pepper

ENCHILADAS

4 cups shredded rotisserie chicken or duck carnitas (see page 225)
¼ cup chicken stock or water
Neutral oil, such as grapeseed or canola, for frying
16 corn tortillas
1⅓ cups grated cheddar and Monterey Jack cheese
⅔ cup grated Gruyère cheese
Chopped cilantro, for garnish
Thinly sliced white onion, soaked in ice water for a few minutes then drained, for garnish

Serves 4

MAKE THE SALSA: Preheat the broiler with a rack 3 to 4 inches from heat. Put the tomatillos, jalapeños, and serranos on a small sheet pan with some space between them and broil, flipping once or twice, until the tomatillos are charred on both sides and completely cooked and the chiles are charred all over, 10 to 15 minutes. Let cool completely.

Transfer the tomatillos and chiles, including any liquid in the pan, to a blender, add the cilantro and garlic, and pulse to a coarse puree. Add the heavy cream, sour cream, salt, granulated bouillon, and pepper and blend until smooth, about 30 seconds. Season to taste with salt and set aside.

MAKE THE ENCHILADAS: In a large skillet, get the chicken and stock hot over medium heat and finely shred the meat. Season to taste with salt and let cool completely.

Preheat the oven to 400°F.

Pour ¼ inch of oil into a small skillet and heat over medium until it shimmers. One by one, cook the tortillas for 10 seconds, just until hot and pliable. As they're done, move them to a cutting board, dab with paper towels, and let cool a little.

One by one, top the tortillas with about ¼ cup of the shredded chicken, roll it up, and put it seam-side down in a 9 by 13-inch baking dish, so it stays rolled. Tuck each rolled tortilla nice and cozy next to the others.

Evenly pour on the salsa to completely cover, sprinkle on both cheeses, and bake until melty and bubbling, 15 to 20 minutes. If you'd like, broil it for a few minutes to get that cheese golden brown.

Sprinkle on some cilantro and onion, and serve hot.

NOTE: A mix of serranos and jalapeños is ideal, delivering the right balance of heat and grassy chile flavor. And a mix of cheeses provides enough complexity to keep the melty topper from tipping into too-much. But you do you.

OYSTER MUSHROOM TAMALES

Shroom-Stuffed Masa, Wrapped 'n' Steamed

Tamales are often a family affair. I've spent countless hours at my grandma's place, especially around Christmas, with my whole fam gathered together in a merry assembly line, laughing and making hundreds of these edible presents gift-wrapped in corn husks. We'd spend days after snacking, heating them up in the microwave or even better, warming them in the husks on a griddle, so they get a little crisp.

Nowadays around the holidays, I make them with my Nixta restaurant fam, but we trade grandma's pork filling for oyster mushrooms stewed in a rich sauce. Other filling options include Chile Colorado (page 84), Duck-Fat Refried Beans (page 241), and Mole Rojo con Pato (page 87).

Equipment: stand mixer, large pot with steamer insert or tamalera (see Note on opposite page)

MUSHROOM FILLING

- 5 dried ancho chiles, stemmed, slit open, and seeded
- 2 dried pasilla chiles, stemmed, slit open, and seeded
- 2 dried guajillo chiles, stemmed, slit open, and seeded
- 6 garlic cloves, peeled but whole
- 8 cups unsalted vegetable stock or chicken stock
- 1 tablespoon ground cumin
- 2 teaspoons dried Mexican oregano
- 2 teaspoons chopped sage
- 3 tablespoons neutral oil, such as grapeseed or canola
- 2 pounds oyster mushrooms, trimmed and torn into thin strips
- Kosher salt
- 2 bay leaves

TAMALES

- 1 pound dried corn husks (hojas para tamal)
- 3 cups cold lard (rendered pork fat) or room-temp vegetable shortening
- 8 cups coarsely ground masa harina (labeled "para tamales"), about 2 pounds
- 4 teaspoons baking powder
- 4 teaspoons Morton kosher salt
- 5 to 6 cups vegetable stock or chicken stock, warmed
- Mexican crema or sour cream, for serving

Makes 40 to 48 tamales

MAKE THE MUSHROOM FILLING: Heat a large dry Dutch oven over medium-high for a minute. Working in batches, toast the chiles, flipping frequently, until aromatic, 1 to 1½ minutes per batch. Transfer to a bowl, cover with hot water (about 8 cups), and soak until soft, about 20 minutes.

In the same pot, cook the garlic, flipping occasionally, until blackened in spots and soft, 6 to 8 minutes.

Drain the chiles, then transfer the chiles and garlic to a blender along with 2 cups of the stock, the cumin, oregano, and sage. Blend until smooth, about 2 minutes. Set aside in the blender for now.

Add the oil to the Dutch oven and heat over medium-high until it shimmers. Working in batches to avoid overcrowding, cook the mushrooms (season lightly with ½ teaspoon salt), flipping once, until golden and slightly crispy on the edges, 4 to 5 minutes per batch. As they're cooked, transfer to a plate and give them another sprinkle of salt.

Return the mushrooms to the pot. Set a fine-mesh sieve over the pot and carefully (it'll splatter!) pour the chile mixture through the sieve, stirring to help it pass through, then discard any solids left behind.

Stir to coat the mushrooms. Add the remaining 6 cups stock and the bay leaves and bring to a simmer. Adjust the heat to cook at a moderate simmer, uncovered and stirring occasionally, until the sauce thickens to coat the mushrooms, 1 to 1½ hours.

Stir in 1½ teaspoons salt or more to taste. Let cool completely before proceeding. (At this point, you can refrigerate for up to 2 days.)

MAKE THE TAMALES: Put the corn husks in a large bowl, cover with hot water, and weigh them down with a plate to submerge. Set aside to soak until floppy-soft, about 1 hour. Drain well and pat dry.

In a stand mixer fitted with the whisk, whisk the lard on low, then gradually increase the speed to high. Mix until the lard has whipped to very soft peaks, 3 to 4 minutes. Turn off the mixer and swap in the paddle attachment. Add the masa harina, baking powder, and salt. Start mixing on low speed and gradually increase to medium-high until you have a shaggy dough, about 2 minutes.

Reduce the speed to low, pour in 5 cups of the warm stock about ½ cup at a time, and mix on medium to make a spreadably soft, slightly sticky dough. Drop a lil' piece of the dough in cold tap water—if it floats, it's ready. If not, mix in another ¼ cup of the stock and try the cold water test again. Cover with a damp kitchen towel.

Choose the biggest 40ish corn husks for making the tamales. Make the tamales one by one: Lay out a corn husk point-side facing away from you. Starting at the bottom, spread the masa to make a roughly 4-inch square, leaving just a tiny border and the top third of the husk empty. Add 2 tablespoons of mushroom filling to the center of the square. Fold the sides of the husk over the filling, then fold the pointed end over the sides, leaving one side open. Flip seam-side down or snip a long piece from the smaller husks and use it to tie up the tamale.

Repeat with the remaining large husks, dough, and filling. If there's any sauciness left over, gently warm it to serve with the tamales.

COOK THE TAMALES: In a large pot with a steamer insert—or even better, a tamalera (see Note)—bring a few inches of water to a boil. The water level should reach just below the base of the steamer or tamalera.

Stand the tamales in the steamer insert open-sides up, starting at the edges to make the task easier. Lower the heat to a gentle simmer, then add the insert and cover with a damp kitchen towel or the remaining husks. Steam for 60 to 70 minutes, topping up with boiling water as needed. To check if they're done, remove a tamal and carefully unfold it—if the husk pulls cleanly away, they're ready.

At this point, you can turn off the heat and let them sit, covered, in the pot for up to 1 hour. When ready to serve, remove from the pot and let cool 10 minutes. (Once fully cooled, the tamales keep frozen in resealable bags for up to 3 months.)

Serve with a drizzle of reserved saucy stuff and dollops of crema.

NOTE: A tamalera is designed for steaming tamales. The narrow pot makes it easy to stand them up, but with some creative leaning and balancing, practically any pot and steamer insert will do. Speaking of being a little flexible, you know what else will do? Chilled duck fat—left over from making the duck carnitas for Duck Carnitas Tacos (page 225)—in place of the lard or shortening.

CHILES EN NOGADA

Stuffed Poblanos 'n' Walnut Sauce

Born in Puebla on the brink of Mexico's independence, this dish wears the colors of the Mexican flag proudly. The story goes that nuns cooking to celebrate victorious army commander Agustín de Iturbide were the creative forces who merged indigenous and colonial ingredients and techniques to make this stunner: roasted green chiles stuffed with a sweet-savory mixture of ground meat, nuts, and fruit, blanketed in white creamy walnut sauce, and scattered with crimson pomegranate seeds. Chiles en nogada is the country's complicated history made delicious.

FILLING

¼ cup neutral oil, such as grapeseed or canola
½ medium white onion, finely chopped
4 garlic cloves, finely chopped
2 pounds ground beef, preferably 80/20
1 tablespoon Morton kosher salt, plus more to taste
1 pound Roma or plum tomatoes, quartered, seeded, and diced
2 cups unsalted beef or chicken stock
1 Granny Smith apple, cored and cut into ¼-inch dice
1 cup blanched whole or sliced almonds, finely chopped
¼ cup golden raisins
1 teaspoon sugar
⅛ teaspoon saffron threads, crushed
⅛ teaspoon ground allspice
⅛ teaspoon ground cinnamon
⅛ teaspoon ground cloves
Freshly ground black pepper

CHILES AND SAUCE

9 large poblano chiles (about 5 ounces each)
1½ cups unsalted roasted pecans (see Note)
1½ cups heavy cream
1½ cups whole milk, plus more as needed
¾ cup cream cheese (6 ounces), at room temp
2 teaspoons Morton kosher salt, plus more to taste

FOR SERVING

Pomegranate seeds
Chopped flat-leaf parsley

Serves 6 to 8

MAKE THE FILLING: Heat the oil in a large skillet over medium-low until it shimmers. Add the onion and cook, stirring occasionally, until softened and translucent, 8 to 10 minutes. Add the garlic and stir for 1 minute.

Increase the heat to medium-high, add the ground beef and salt, and cook, stirring and breaking up clumps, until any water that comes out evaporates and the meat is fully cooked, 10 to 12 minutes.

Add the tomatoes and beef stock and bring to a simmer. Adjust the heat to simmer steadily, uncovered, until the liquid is mostly absorbed, 20 to 25 minutes.

Stir in the apple, almonds, raisins, sugar, saffron, allspice, cinnamon, cloves, and pepper to taste. Simmer, stirring frequently, until the apple is tender but not mushy, about 10 minutes. Season to taste with salt. Let cool slightly. (Keeps in the fridge for up to 3 days. Gently rewarm before you continue.)

CHAR THE CHILES: Preheat the oven broiler with a rack 3 to 4 inches from heat. Put the chiles on a large sheet pan with some space between them and broil, flipping twice, until blistered and charred all over, 15 to 20 minutes.

Transfer to a baking dish in a single layer, cover tightly, and let them chill out for 10 minutes, until they're cool enough to handle. Being careful to keep the chiles intact, scrape off the charred skins (no rinsing!), then make a lengthwise slit in each chile. There's no need to remove the seeds.

Gently spoon the beef mixture into each chile, taking care not to tear them. No need to close them back up. Set aside at room temperature while you make the sauce.

MAKE THE SAUCE: Up to 1 hour before serving, in a blender, combine the pecans, cream, milk, cream cheese, and salt and blend until silky smooth. If necessary, thin with a splash of milk to the consistency of thick heavy cream. Season with salt to taste.

TO SERVE: Transfer the stuffed chiles to plates or a platter, then spoon the pecan sauce over the top. Garnish with pomegranate seeds and chopped parsley. Serve at room temperature.

NOTE: Walnuts are classic, but we in Texas, so it's pecans for us!

CHILE COLORADO

Red Chile Pork Stew

This smoky, spicy, and herbaceous dish of simmered pork might remind you of Texas chili. And that's no coincidence. No doubt that Tejanos cooking this classic guisado (stew in Spanish) influenced those pots of Texas red—colorado, after all, is just another word for rojo. Whether you call it chili or guisado, just remember that beans in the pot are an absolute hell to the naw.

STEW

- 5 dried ancho chiles, stemmed but whole
- 2 dried guajillo chiles, stemmed but whole
- 2 dried New Mexico chiles or pasilla chiles, stemmed but whole
- 4 pounds boneless, skinless pork shoulder, cut into 2-inch pieces
- ¼ cup vegetable oil, plus more if needed
- Morton kosher salt and freshly ground black pepper
- 8 cups unsalted chicken stock
- 6 garlic cloves, minced
- 1 tablespoon finely chopped sage
- 1 tablespoon ground cumin
- 1 teaspoon dried Mexican oregano
- 2 bay leaves

FOR SERVING

- Lots of corn tortillas
- Thinly sliced red onion
- Chopped cilantro
- Lime wedges

Serves 6 to 8

MAKE THE STEW: Heat a large Dutch oven over medium-high for a minute. Working in batches, toast the chiles, flipping frequently, until fragrant, 1 to 2 minutes per batch. Transfer to a bowl, cover with hot water, and weigh them down to submerge. Set aside for 20 minutes to soften the chiles.

Meanwhile, pat the pork dry. In the same large pot, heat the oil over medium-high and let it get a lil' smoky. Working in batches, season the pork generously with salt and pepper and brown the pork, turning occasionally, for 8 to 10 minutes per batch. Transfer the browned pork to a sheet pan, leaving the fat in the pot. If the pot is dry, add a splash of oil.

When the chiles have softened, drain them, discarding the soaking liquid. Transfer the chiles to a blender, add 3 cups of the stock, and blend until smooth, 1 to 2 minutes. Set aside.

Remove the pot from the heat, add the garlic and sage, and cook with the residual heat, stirring, until fragrant, about 1 minute. Add the cumin and oregano and stir until fragrant. Add 1 cup of the stock, return the pot to the heat, and bring to a simmer over medium, scraping up any browned bits from the pot with a wooden spoon.

Add the pork, bay leaves, chile puree, 1 tablespoon of salt, and the remaining 4 cups stock (swish some around the blender to get all the chile puree) and stir well. Bring to a boil over high heat. Cover the pot, lower the heat to cook at a gentle simmer for about 1 hour, until the pork is tender. Uncover the pot, increase the heat to cook at a moderate simmer until the liquid has thickened enough to coat the back of a spoon, about 45 minutes more. Season with salt and pepper to taste.

TO SERVE: When the pork's almost done, warm and hold the tortillas (see how on page 38). Serve topped with red onion and cilantro and with lime wedges and tortillas on the side.

NOTE: The stew tastes better the next day, so feel free to (or maybe even plan to) make it in advance, so the flavors can meld in the fridge.

MOLE ROJO CON PATO

Oaxacan Red Chile Sauce 'n' Duck—aka Mexican Fesenjoon

This is a celebration mole. Not all moles are complex, but when my grandmother had the whole fam at her house, she'd go all out, toasting a million dried chiles and fruits and nuts and spices. The aromas coming from her kitchen, as we all hung and chatted and laughed in the living room, were unforgettable. We streamline the method here, roasting everything in the oven. So really, the only lift is collecting the (many) ingredients and making sure you lean into the char.

Serve the mole with plenty of warm tortillas for mopping up every bit of the sauce.

MOLE ROJO

- 1 corn tortilla
- 15 dried pasilla chiles (5 ounces), stemmed, slit open, and seeded
- 4 dried ancho chiles, stemmed, slit open, and seeded
- 3 tablespoons raw pecans or walnuts
- 2 tablespoons raw almonds
- 2 tablespoons black or white sesame seeds
- 2 tablespoons unsalted roasted peanuts
- 1 allspice berry
- 1 star anise
- 1 small stick canela (Mexican cinnamon)
- 1 whole clove
- 1 sprig thyme
- 1 sprig oregano
- 1 tablespoon ground ginger
- ¼ teaspoon ground nutmeg
- 8 ounces Roma or plum tomatoes, halved
- 2 large garlic cloves, unpeeled
- 2 prunes
- ½ medium white onion, quartered
- ¼ super-ripe (black) plantain, peeled and sliced ½ inch thick
- 1 tablespoon raisins
- 2 cups unsalted chicken stock
- 2 cups water

ASSEMBLY

- 3 tablespoons neutral oil, such as grapeseed or canola
- 8 ounces Mexican chocolate (2½ tablets), roughly chopped
- 2 tablespoons Morton kosher salt
- 4 to 6 whole cooked duck legs from Duck Carnitas Tacos (page 225)
- So many corn tortillas
- White sesame seeds, for garnish

Serves 4 to 6

MAKE THE MOLE ROJO: Preheat the oven to 450°F. Position an oven rack in the center and another in the bottom position.

Over a stovetop flame, cook the tortilla, flipping occasionally, until crisp and almost totally blackened, about 3 minutes. Break into several pieces and set aside.

On a large sheet pan, arrange the chiles, burnt tortilla, pecans, almonds, sesame seeds, and peanuts in a more or less single layer. To an empty part of the pan, add the allspice, star anise, canela, clove, thyme, oregano, ginger, and nutmeg in a low pile. On a separate large sheet pan, arrange the tomatoes, garlic, prunes, onion, plantain, and raisins in a single layer.

Put the sheet pan with the chiles on the center rack and roast until the chiles are burnt and the spices and nuts are nice and dark, about 12 minutes. Put the sheet pan with the tomatoes on the bottom rack and roast, flipping once, until well charred, 25 to 30 minutes.

Working in 2 batches, blend the roasted ingredients with the chicken stock and water until very smooth, 2 to 3 minutes.

ASSEMBLE THE DISH: Heat the oil in a large skillet over medium until it shimmers. Add the mole and immediately partially cover to block splatter. Swish a little water in the blender to access any lingering mole and add it to the pot. Decrease the heat and simmer gently, stirring frequently, until it thickens slightly, 10 to 15 minutes.

Stir in the chocolate and salt and cook, partially covered and stirring and scraping occasionally, for 30 minutes more, to meld the flavors. As you cook, gradually add more water if necessary to maintain a pourable, velvety consistency. Season with more salt to taste. (At this point, you can let it cool and refrigerate for up to 4 days. It gets even better as it sits. Before serving, gently heat, gradually adding water as needed.)

Meanwhile, if the duck legs are freshly made, remove them from the fat just before serving. Otherwise, heat them over medium-low heat in a pan with some of the duck fat, flipping once, until a little crispy and hot through.

Warm and hold the tortillas (see how on page 38).

Spoon the mole onto serving plates. Top with the duck legs and some more mole, garnish with sesame seeds, and serve with warm tortillas.

SALSAS, PICKLES, DRINKS, AND STUFF

AVOCADO CREMA

Crema without the cream, this silky puree of avocado has just the right amount of salt and acid to give the buttery fruit some POW. You can just slather it on anything, but we often transfer it to a piping or resealable plastic bag, twist to force it toward a corner, then snip off the corner. Snip perpendicular to that first cut and pipe away for a fancy look for Beet "Tartare" Tostadas (page 209) and Chilaquiles Rojos (page 45).

6 medium Hass avocados
½ cup plus 2 tablespoons fresh lime juice (5 to 8 limes)
2½ teaspoons Morton kosher salt

Makes about 4 cups

Pit and peel the avocados, then roughly chop them. Put them in a medium bowl, add the lime juice and salt, and using an immersion blender, blend until smooth and creamy. A regular blender works, too, if you're willing to stir and prod to get it all going and to get in there after blending to scrape out the crema. (Keeps in a container with plastic wrap pressed against the surface to prevent oxidation in the fridge for up to 2 days.)

AVOCADO SALSA

Creamy, bright, with a little heat, this is salsa or, depending how you look at life, a pourable guacamole. It's meant for the torta on page 57, but it's welcome almost anywhere.

1 medium Hass avocado
2 tablespoons finely chopped white onion
1 tablespoon chopped cilantro
½ jalapeño chile, seeded and finely chopped
1 teaspoon Morton kosher salt, plus more to taste
Juice of 2 limes, plus more to taste

Makes ⅔ cup

Halve and pit the avocado. Scoop the avocado flesh into a medium mixing bowl, mash until creamy but still chunky. Stir in the onion, cilantro, jalapeño, salt, and lime juice. If necessary, gradually stir in water until pourable and season to taste with salt and lime juice. It's best enjoyed within an hour or so.

SALSA CRUDA

Raw Tomatillo and Serrano Salsa

This blend-and-go condiment showcases the simplicity of Mexican salsas and the vibrancy of cruda ("raw") ingredients. Cilantro is herbaceous, the chiles are grassy and sharp, and the bright acidity of tomatillos gets revved up with lime juice. A little oil drizzled in at the tail end of blending adds a little body. The salsa cuts the richness of Duck Carnitas Tacos (page 225), amplifies quiet Migas Tacos (page 190), and adds that oh-damn factor to Smash Burgers al Pastor (page 205).

We hack the umami with the highly nontraditional but very much welcome addition of fish sauce. The Squid brand is our pick, but any Thai or Vietnamese product with a nice balance of sweetness and saltiness works.

8 ounces tomatillos (4 to 6), husked, rinsed, and quartered
1 serrano chile, roughly chopped
1 garlic clove, peeled
½ jalapeño chile, roughly chopped
½ bunch of cilantro, bottoms trimmed
¼ medium yellow onion, roughly chopped
¼ cup fresh lime juice (3 to 4 limes)
1½ teaspoons fish sauce or tamari
1½ teaspoons Morton kosher salt
¼ cup neutral oil, such as grapeseed or canola

Makes about 1¾ cups

In a blender, combine everything except the oil and blend on high until the mixture is completely smooth and the color is a solid bright green, about 2 minutes. With the blender still running, slowly pour in the oil. (Keeps in the fridge for up to 2 days.)

SALSA MORITA

Smoky Chipotle Salsa

Little purplish chipotles (aka moritas) are the stars here, with their smoky flavor and their oof heat. Roasted tomatillos provide tang and body while onions and garlic add roundness and a touch of sweetness to this silky smooth salsa. It amps up our Bean and Cheese Tacos (page 222) and turns tortilla chips into next-level Chilaquiles Rojos (page 45).

4 dried chipotle chiles (moritas)
8 ounces tomatillos (4 to 6), husked, rinsed, and quartered
3 garlic cloves, peeled
1 medium yellow onion, quartered and peeled
1 tablespoon apple cider vinegar, plus more to taste
2 teaspoons demerara or granulated sugar
½ teaspoon Morton kosher salt, plus more to taste

Makes about 2 cups

In a small saucepan, combine the chiles with enough water to cover by 2 inches. Bring to a boil over high heat and cook until the chiles are super soft but not falling apart, about 15 minutes. Drain well.

Meanwhile, preheat the broiler with a rack 3 to 4 inches from heat. Put the tomatillos, garlic, and onion on a small sheet pan with some space between them and broil, flipping once or twice, until softened and well charred, 10 to 15 minutes for the garlic and tomatillos and up to 20 minutes for the onion. Let cool slightly.

Transfer the chiles, charred veg, vinegar, sugar, and salt to a blender and blend on high until it's completely smooth (no seeds left!), 1 to 2 minutes. If necessary, gradually add water until the salsa is pourable but still quite thick. Season to taste with vinegar and salt. (Keeps in the fridge for up to 6 days or in the freezer for up to 3 months.)

SALSA MACHA

Mexican Chile Crisp

Veracruz's answer to Chinese chili crisp, this deeply flavored oil-based salsa is packed with mild, fruity chiles, garlic, and nuts. It's good on everything, particularly seafood—for example, fish tacos (see page 62)—but also with nopales (see page 58) and on our meatless tostadas featuring beets (see page 209), carrots (see page 218), and eggs (see page 193).

2 cups neutral oil, such as grapeseed or canola
3 dried ancho chiles, stemmed, seeded, and snipped into pieces with scissors
2 dried pasilla or New Mexico chiles, stemmed, seeded, and snipped
2 dried guajillo chiles, stemmed, seeded, and snipped
¼ cup raw pecans, finely chopped
2 tablespoons raw sesame seeds
3 garlic cloves, roughly chopped
½ teaspoon dried Mexican oregano
1 tablespoon apple cider vinegar
1½ teaspoons Morton kosher salt

Makes about 2½ cups

In a medium saucepan, combine the oil, chiles, pecans, sesame seeds, and garlic. Set it over medium heat and let the oil start to bubble, 6 to 7 minutes. Cook, stirring frequently, until the garlic is lightly golden, about 8 minutes. Remove from the heat, stir in the oregano, and let it cool to room temperature, about 30 minutes.

Transfer to a food processor, add the vinegar and salt, and process until almost completely smooth with some sesame seeds still visible throughout the salsa, 2 to 3 minutes.

The salsa is great right away, but it gets even better as it sits in the fridge. For best results, let it sit in the fridge for at least 1 week. (Keeps in the fridge for up to 3 months.)

SALSA DE CHILTEPÍN

Spicy-Ass Salsa

This simple salsa—thin like hot sauce—features what some historians call the "mother of all chiles." OG status aside, chiltepín is special because of its size (itty-bitty and spherical, the size of petite peas) and distinctive flavor: super citrusy not to mention hot as fuck. It's meant for drizzling on carne asada (see page 65), but it belongs anywhere your go-to hot sauce would go.

½ cup diced white onion
¼ cup dried chiltepínes (tepin chiles)
12 garlic cloves, roughly chopped
4 tablespoons neutral oil, such as grapeseed or canola
1 cup apple cider vinegar
½ cup water
2 teaspoons Morton kosher salt

Makes about 2 cups

In a small saucepan, combine the onion, chiles, garlic, and 2 tablespoons of the oil. Cook over medium-low heat until the onion softens slightly, about 5 minutes.

Add the vinegar, water, and salt, increase the heat to high, and simmer vigorously for 4 minutes to soften the chiles.

Remove from the heat, let cool slightly, then blend with the remaining 2 tablespoons oil until mostly smooth. Let cool completely. (Keeps in the fridge for up to 10 days.)

SALSA DE HABANERO

Spiciest-Ass Salsa

This salsa is fire, in both senses of the word. That is, it's really good—a creamy aioli-like emulsion full of the habanero's one-of-a-kind floral flavor—and it's brutally hot. Tongue-scaldingly, booty-clenchingly, pain-as-pleasure hot, and balanced—just barely—by the sweetness of the onions, garlic, and chiles charring in bubbling oil. Try it on Migas Tacos (page 190), Duck Carnitas Tacos (page 225), Tacos de Pescado (page 62), and Tacos de Cochinita Pibil (page 68).

Warning: When things heat up, you may want to wear a Hazmat suit (okay, a kitchen towel over your mouth and nose is fine), because the air in your place is about to get spicy.

- 1½ cups neutral oil, such as grapeseed or canola
- 8 ounces orange habanero chiles (about 20), stemmed but whole
- 6 garlic cloves, peeled but whole
- 1 large yellow onion, cut into 1-inch dice
- 1 Roma or plum tomato, quartered
- 2 teaspoons Morton kosher salt, plus more to taste
- 2 tablespoons demerara or granulated sugar

Makes about 2 cups

In a medium saucepan, combine the oil, habaneros, garlic, and onion. Set over medium-high heat and cook, stirring and scraping the pan occasionally, until the chiles, garlic, and onion are deep golden in spots, 15 to 20 minutes.

Add the tomato and cook until softened, 2 to 3 minutes. Turn off the heat and let it cool for 15 minutes or so.

Transfer to a blender, add the salt and sugar, and blend on high until smooth and mayo-like, about 2 minutes. Season to taste with salt. (Keeps in the fridge for up to 1 week.)

PICO DE GALLO

A classic pico de gallo, plus a slight variation made with cherry tomatoes (see below) that's just the thing for Huaraches de Nopales (page 58) and really, anything that yearns for fresh, bright contrast. Both versions feature the keys to good pico: aggressive seasoning (a small spoonful should make a big impact) and letting the salsa sit for a bit before eating, so the flavors have a chance to come together.

- 1 cup diced tomato, preferably heirloom
- 2 tablespoons finely chopped white onion
- 1 serrano or jalapeño chile, minced (seeded if you scared), plus more to taste
- 1 tablespoon chopped cilantro
- 1 tablespoon fresh lime juice, plus more to taste
- ½ teaspoon Morton kosher salt, plus more to taste

Makes about 1 cup

In a medium serving bowl, combine the tomato, onion, chile, cilantro, lime juice, and salt. Let sit at room temperature for at least 10 minutes to allow the flavors to meld. Season to taste with more chile, lime, and salt. You want it punchy.

Serve with a slotted spoon, leaving most of the juices behind.

CHERRY TOMATO PICO DE GALLO

Replace the heirloom tomatoes with 1 cup cherry tomatoes, quartered. Use red onion instead of white and increase the amount to ¼ cup. Increase the cilantro to 2 tablespoons. The chile, lime juice, and salt all stay the same. Let sit as directed.

ESCABECHE

Pickled Veg—aka Mexican Shoori

This easy-peasy, snackable Mexican pickle contains crunchy carrots, cauliflower, and jalapeños. It adds a nice pop of acidity and heat when served alongside any rich dish, from Tortas de Milanesa (page 57) to Mama Rico's Chorizo Meatloaf (page 75).

1½ cups sliced (¼-inch rounds) peeled carrots
3 cups 1-inch cauliflower florets
6 garlic cloves, peeled but whole
2 jalapeño chiles, cut into ¼-inch rounds
3 bay leaves
1 tablespoon dried Mexican oregano
1½ teaspoons black peppercorns
3 cups water
1½ cups distilled white vinegar
2 tablespoons Morton kosher salt
1½ tablespoons demerara or granulated sugar

Makes about 2 quarts

In a large bowl, toss together the carrots, cauliflower, garlic, jalapeños, bay leaves, oregano, and peppercorns. Transfer to a 2-quart heatproof jar or divide between two heatproof 1-quart jars.

In a medium saucepan, combine the water, vinegar, salt, and sugar and bring to a boil, stirring to completely dissolve the salt and sugar. Pour the hot mixture into the jar(s) to submerge the veg, and set aside at least 1 hour to cool and pickle before covering or eating. If the vegetables float, a folded paper towel on the surface of the brine helps keep them submerged. (Keeps in the fridge for up to 1 month.)

PICKLED RED ONIONS

These pickles are remixed with xnipec, a condiment that's a staple in the Yucatán and whose name means "dog's nose" in the Mayan language, because the heat of habanero will make your nose wet like one. They're an essential partner for Tacos de Cochinita Pibil (page 68), but we use them far and wide.

1 large red onion, sliced ⅛ inch thick
1½ teaspoons Morton kosher salt
½ cup fresh lime juice (4 to 6 limes)
½ cup apple cider vinegar
1 teaspoon dried Mexican oregano
1 habanero chile, seeded and finely minced

Makes about 2 cups

In a medium bowl, combine the onion and salt, toss well, and set aside for 5 minutes. Add the lime juice, vinegar, oregano, and habanero and stir well. Transfer everything to a narrow container (it's best if the liquid mostly covers the solids).

Cover and let pickle in the fridge for at least 2 hours or, for an electric-pink color, overnight. After an hour or so, stir and press on the solids so they're submerged. (Keeps in the fridge for up to 1 month.)

TEPACHE

Pre-Hispanic Pineapple Drank

You, too, can turn skin-on pineapple, ginger, and cloves into a slightly alcoholic effervescent tropical bevvy—it's Mexico's kombucha, but if you ask us, it's way better. The secret is *not* rinsing the pineapple, so the natural yeasts on the peel can work their magic.

Equipment: 1½- to 2-gallon glass jar, cheesecloth, enough jars or bottles with swing-top lids to hold 4 quarts

8 ounces piloncillo (see page 18)
4 cinnamon sticks
2 habanero chiles, stemmed but whole
1-inch knob of ginger, unpeeled and sliced
8 cups water
1 ripe pineapple (not rinsed or washed!)

Makes about 4 quarts

Whack the piloncillo (still in the plastic packaging) with a pestle or heavy pan to break it into several pieces. In a medium pot, combine the piloncillo, cinnamon, chiles, ginger, and water. Bring to a boil, stirring occasionally, until the sugar has completely dissolved.

Meanwhile, slice off and discard the top and bottom of the pineapple but keep the peel on. Cut the pineapple (including the core) into 1 by 1-inch chunks and transfer to a clean 1½- to 2-gallon glass jar.

Once the sugar has dissolved, pour the mixture into the container with the pineapple, stir well, and cover with cheesecloth. Put the container in a warm (about 75°F), dark, draft-free area (maybe the cupboard or above the fridge) for 4 days. Spot a little white-ish film on the surface? Chill, that's just yeast. Skim it off before proceeding.

Pour the liquid through a fine-mesh sieve into clean jars or bottles with swing-top lids, discarding any remaining solids (or trimming off the peel and saving the pineapple for the tepache salsa on page 74). Tightly cover with the lids and leave it out again for 2 days.

Finally, refrigerate overnight—it'll get effervescent. (Keeps in the fridge for up to 1 week. Every 2 or 3 days, "burp" the tepache—aka remove the lid for 10 seconds and then reclose—so it doesn't, uh, explode.)

MICHELADAS

Mexican Bloody Marys

There's the simple Mexican classic: beer, ice, and lime juice, served in a glass with a salt rim. And then there's this, the party version that has taken off 'round these parts—you know, the one with Bloody Mary vibes. Ours is extra special, welcoming tomatoes and celery buzzed with Worcestershire and hot sauce to the glass. There's Tajín on the rim, of course, which sticks thanks to lime or chamoy, the sweet-sour Mexican condiment. Long live tangy, spicy, salty cold beer.

Light Mexican lager—Modelo Especial, Tecate, et al.—is the move.

MICHELADA MIX

3 Roma or plum tomatoes
1½ cups chopped (½ inch) celery
Generous ¼ cup diced yellow onion
¾ cup Old Bay hot sauce or Crystal hot sauce
½ cup Nixta's Fresno Hot Sauce (page 239) or sriracha
2½ tablespoons Worcestershire sauce
1 tablespoon fresh lime juice
¾ teaspoon Japanese soy sauce or tamari
¾ teaspoon Morton kosher salt

MICHELADAS

Tajín (optional), for serving
Juice of 1 lime or chamoy (optional)
Ice cubes
About 6 Mexican beers

Makes 8 drinks

MAKE THE MICHELADA MIX: Bring about 4 cups water to a boil in a small pot. Add the tomatoes, celery, and onion, then lower the heat to cook at a gentle simmer until they're nice and soft but the tomatoes are still intact, 15 to 20 minutes. Drain the vegetables, discarding the liquid.

In a blender, combine the hot sauces, Worcestershire sauce, lime juice, soy sauce, and salt. Add the drained veg and blend on high until completely smooth, about 1 minute. Let cool completely.

Refrigerate until fully chilled, at least 2 hours. (At this point, the michelada mix can be refrigerated for up to 1 week.)

MAKE THE MICHELADAS: For Tajín rims, dump a nice layer of Tajín on a small plate. Moisten the rim of each pint glass with lime juice or chamoy, then invert each glass onto the Tajín, giving it a little twisty-twist to coat.

Fill each pint glass with ice cubes, pour in ½ cup of Michelada mix, and top with beer. Drink, topping up with beer as you do.

HORCHATA

Rice Milk 'n' Cinnamon Drank

To cool your palate alongside spicy food, nothing beats horchata, the milky but milkless classic. Think the flavors of Mexican cinnamon–spiked rice pudding distilled into a cold drink.

Equipment: Cheesecloth

8 cups water
2 cups jasmine rice
1 cup demerara or granulated sugar
6 inches canela (Mexican cinnamon), in two pieces

Makes 8 drinks

In a large container, combine the water, rice, sugar, and cinnamon and stir well. Cover and let soak overnight in the fridge.

Line a strainer with cheesecloth. Give the mix a good stir, then blend in two batches on high speed until smooth, 1 to 3 minutes, depending on your blender. Pour each batch through the strainer into a pitcher, stirring to extract the liquid, then discarding the solids after each batch. (Keeps in the fridge for up to 3 days. Stir really well before serving.)

Serve in glasses over ice.

CHAMPURRADO

Mexican Hot Chocolate

Cold nights are perfect for this version of atole, just one star in the vast sky of hot masa-enriched drinks that date back to the Aztecs and Mayans. Known as champurrado, this one is flavored with chocolate, allspice, and Mexican cinnamon. The earthy masa balances the slight sweetness a bit and every sip is like a warm hug.

7 cups water
¾ cup demerara or granulated sugar
2 teaspoons allspice berries
4 to 6 inches canela (Mexican cinnamon), in two pieces
5 whole cloves
6½ ounces Mexican chocolate (aka 2 discs of Abuelita), very roughly chopped
¾ cup masa harina, preferably heirloom corn

Serves 6

In a large pot, combine the water, sugar, allspice, cinnamon, and cloves and bring to a full boil over high heat. Lower the heat to simmer steadily for 20 minutes, to infuse the spices.

Start whisking, then add the chocolate, piece by piece, until the chocolate has completely melted. Keep on whisking as you gradually pour in the masa harina in a steady stream. Cook at a gentle simmer, stirring occasionally, until it thickens, about 5 minutes. If necessary, gradually add more water until the mixture is eggnog thick.

Pour the mixture through a sieve into a clean pot or thermos, discarding the solids. Cover to keep hot until ready to serve, up to 1 hour.

جویده یابنده

Aghebat jooyande yabande bovad

"The seeker will always find their way."

—FARHAD "FRED" MARDANBIGI
(THAT'S MY BABA)

IRAN

RECIPES FROM THE MOTHERLAND

دارچین
KASHK
MIZAN
SAFFRON

SOMEHOW, SOME WAY, THEY DID IT. My parents came to America as young adults, leaving behind everything and everyone, and arriving to nothing and no one.

Born in Tehran, my maman (that's mom) and baba (that's dad) landed in Maryland, then hit up South Carolina, and settled in Springdale, Arkansas, where Baba went to study agricultural engineering. Several years after she arrived, Maman found herself with four kids, a few friends, and very little English. She cooked like her life depended on it. She cooked to hold on to her home, even though, both geographically and culturally, she was about a million miles away. Maman cooked to feed us, to feed herself, and to show us where we came from.

My childhood mornings smelled like onions frying, like fenugreek leaves and smuggled saffron—for Maman, only the good stuff from Iran would do. By 6 a.m., wearing her signature red lipstick, with her perfectly coiffed hair and six spritzes of her perfume of the week (she had dozens to choose from), she'd be presiding over three weathered Walmart pots. She still uses them religiously, preferring them to All-Clad and Le Creuset.

One pot might have contained Ghormeh Sabzi (page 156), beef slowly stewing with black dried limes, yellow turmeric, and huge handfuls of chopped green herbs; or Fesenjoon (page 159) made with chicken or lil' meatballs (aka ghelghely) simmered with fruit and nuts. Two decades later, I'd be eating mole in Austin with Edgar and think to myself, *This reminds me of fesenjoon*. Maman learned to cook in part because she could not suffer her sister's food. My khaleh (aunt) Azam is a woman of many talents—she designs clothing that would rival any on a *Vogue* cover—but cooking is not one of them. Maman continues to rag on her mushy rice to this day.

Maman cooked Iranian food six days a week. The seventh day she made "American" food. Cheesy beans (green beans from the can topped with three slices of Kraft American cheese and microwaved), spaghetti with ketchup, and eggs with weenies.

I grew up with that same out-of-place feeling so many first-gen immigrants have. We were, at least for a while, the only Iranians in town. In fact, when most people first saw us, they took in our swarthiness and spoke to us in Spanish. It was an educated guess—a solid chunk of the town was Latino, many there to toil in chicken processing at Tyson HQ.

Spanish didn't do the trick, but for a while, English wouldn't have been much better. My parents spoke Farsi at home, so until kindergarten I spoke approximately zero English. Between this and Mom packing me Kotlet (page 136) or ghormeh sabzi for lunch, the sense of unbelonging was wild. It peaked when I auditioned to be a cowgirl for the Kindergarten Circus, but got the part of the bear. While a gaggle of blondies jaunted around the stage on stick horses, there I was in a cage, crammed into a furry jumper and wearing a red tutu my mom had sewn. At the after-party in the cafeteria, I looked at the dino nuggets and square pizza and thought, *No more ghormeh sabzi. I want this*.

Being Iranian was a lot. On TV, we were depicted as bogeymen—primitive, backward, terrorists. Meanwhile, Baba's main occupation was going on about how Iranians invented everything. And Maman expressed her Persian nature by coaxing cashiers to give her discounts. I'd have to translate, because they either couldn't understand her heavy accent or why she was asking for a discount on an item that was already discounted—or more likely, both. I just wanted not to feel so *foreign*.

I felt foreign where I was born and where I was "from." Every summer, Maman lugged her four babies to Iran for three full months. The five of us flew from Fayetteville, Arkansas, to Dallas to NYC to Frankfurt to Kuwait to Tehran. We'd arrive to a frenetic horde of family, swarming and yelling like paparazzi. These were the cousins, aunts, uncles, real and deputized, who would cram us into cars and whisk us to Darrous, a quiet old neighborhood in the city of nearly fourteen million. En route, we got a taste of the world-famous Iranian driving—mopeds heaving with families of five (plus a sheep), a maelstrom of honking and hand gestures, five rows of cars in two lanes.

As a kid, trips to Tehran were both sweet and brutal. Sweet to know I had so much family (not that I always recognized them all). Sweet to raid the trees in my agha joon's (grandpa's) backyard for tiny sour cherries, apricots, and plums, which my aunts and grandma cooked down either for jam or spread on

After a daylong goose chase with some down-to-clown strangers, we finally found my Mamani's tea farm in Lahijan.

My Khaleh Azam has carried around this dried-ass salted fish with her for over sixty years! She calls it her spirit animal since they are both mahi sefids (whitefish). Pure joy this petrified fish brings her (lol).

trays and dried on the roof to make lavashak, the OG Fruit Roll-Ups. Brutal because I felt almost equally out of place. In Springdale, my English was a work in progress. In Tehran, my Farsi was a work without progress. That's me, Sara Mardanbigi, embarrassing herself at home and abroad. Brutal, too, because we were shuttled from home to home for seemingly ceaseless mehmoonis (house parties) at which my siblings and I were subjected to taarof, the demented art of Persian hospitality.

Taarof is, essentially, a fierce, relentless generosity competition, a game of chicken between provider and recipient. It's complimenting someone's bra only to have them, quite literally, remove it then and there and hand it to you, while you tenderly and aggressively decline the offering as if your pride depended on it. (And yes, this actually happened.) It's the warzone of politeness that ensues after Maman pops open the two giant, stuffed suitcases she hauled to Iran and starts gifting their contents—perfume, makeup, shirts, shoes, and other fruits of all that aforementioned haggling—all of which must be vehemently rejected before it can be accepted.

Along with illicit saffron, Maman sneaked taarof into Arkansas. In Iranian culture, food and hospitality are inextricably linked, so the dementedness extends to the kitchen. Edgar and I visited her once around his birthday and she had cooked a twenty-dish feast. When we asked who else was coming to celebrate with us, she looked at the two of us and said, matter-of-factly, This is everyone. In Iran and at Maman's home in Arkansas, any moment you weren't eating—despite how much you had already eaten—you might be accosted with yet another plate of kabob, khoresht, and rice, rice, rice.

Maman's rice game is strong, the fluffiness the stuff of legend. I've watched her make rice a thousand times. I know that she soaks the rice in water that's Dead Sea–level salty. I know that during the first cook, she doesn't just dump in the rice but adds it in small handfuls, so that, in the words of Maman, "the grains can dance around each other in the water." I know that during the second cook she adds the rice not in an even layer but in a gently sloping hill and uses the back of a wooden spoon to make six deep wells to let the steam escape. This is the craft of making rice, the steps I've learned to trace, that allows a simple grain to transcend its humble purpose. Then there's the art, the lil' moves that come from making it thousands of times.

Growing up in Arkansas, rice kept us tethered to our roots. It was there for virtually every meal, even Thanksgiving. Our family tradition dictates that every year, we snap a photo of Maman dangling a raw turkey by the wings and absolutely beaming over the arrival of her favorite holiday. Her table was thoroughly American—the roasted bird, boxed stuffing, canned corn, and cheesy beans. (In college, I brought cheesy beans to a Thanksgiving potluck, as if it were the most natural thing in the world, like bringing stuffing or sweet potatoes. The looks I got!) Without fail, however, this spread included a golden heap of saffron rice.

The older I got, the more interested I became in the twists and turns of these roots, and the more my parents shifted from avatars of Iran to, just, people. I began to wonder about them, what brought them to America and what they might have sacrificed in the process. Though my trips to Iran became fewer and farther between, I found myself a more active participant, those mehmoonis less a burden and more an opportunity to piece together their story. Like many first-genners, I spent so much of my life running away from my culture. I was finally ready to run toward it.

This shift culminated in a trip to Iran in 2023. I hadn't been as a grown-ass adult. I had never been there with Baba or Edgar. This trip would be a trip.

Unlike Maman, Baba wasn't a homebody nor did he abide taarof. So instead of family musical chairs in Tehran, we traversed the entire country, which is stop-in-your-tracks beautiful. Our one-month, twenty-city tour took us to Qeshm, a subtropical southern island in the Strait of Hormuz, where we woke in complete silence save for the rustling of date trees. To my Baba Joon's ancestral home of Yazd, a parched city in central Iran cooled by ancient badgirs (wind catchers) and furnished by qanat (underground aqueducts). To the nearby town of Mehriz—from the word mehr (kindness) and riz (bleeding), because the people there are said to bleed kindness—where the Mardanbigi surname originated and where I almost peed my pants during a gravity-defying ride in a 1980 Nissan Patrol through snowy desert.

The whole time, Edgar was Edgar. Even though he knew four words in Farsi, he somehow made friends with everyone, even the Iranian men's basketball team, which he discovered towering over the rest of us at the Bandar Abbas airport. And he ate like a madman—the sambusa (the OG samosa) in Qeshm, aush mast (yogurt soup drizzled with fried mint oil) in the mountain town of Masouleh, breads the size of prayer rugs, and a surprising number of hot dogs, including a snappy, spicy number topped with caviar.

And Baba was Baba. Lean and modestly dressed, he sported a luxuriant 'stache and swagger for days. He was dispensing Baba-isms ("Illegal is a sick bird"—get it: ill, eagle?), cracking his off-color jokes that somehow fly, and serving as highly partisan tour guide, marveling at historical sites while reminding us that Iranians invented, well, everything (horses! math!). As always, he was as generous with his funds and Mr. Fix-It skills (he loves sneaky-paying for dinner and mending a friend's muffler) as he was guarded with his emotions—at least until we reached Tehran to visit my dayee (uncle) Asghar. Dayee Asghar and Baba had long ago made mischief together. Yet now, in the final stages of Parkinson's, Dayee could hardly walk or talk, and Baba cried as they embraced after so many years apart.

Then, toward the end of the trip, there was Gilan, a region in the shomal (north) that abuts the shores of the Caspian Sea and is the heart of Iranian gastronomy. This is not the baked Iran of the American imagination but a lush sliver that's home to vast grids of swampy rice paddies, dewy forests, and snow-capped mountains with homes carved into the sides. At last, we reached the sleepy town of Langaroud. It was a homecoming of sorts, my baba's return after ten years and my first time ever visiting the place where his mother and my mamani, the late Soghrah Tayabeh aka Mamani Iran, was born.

Our culinary matriarch was born here in rice country, which grows 85 percent of the nation's total crop. While the history, as usual, is a bit murky, rice was probably introduced to Iran around the fourth century BCE and took more than one thousand years and an Arab conquest for it to take off. In the arid regions of Iran, bread is still common, but here in the north, a meal isn't a meal, as Mamani used to say, without rice.

Mamani wasn't there this time—she was ensconced in Baltimore, where she'd pass a year later—but my memories of her were everywhere. There she was in her signature understated but exquisite headscarf, small in stature and giant in spirit. There she was perched on a chair, gazing at her sprawling family and beaming. There she was in her garden, crooning at her pet chicken and dutifully smashing eggs on the ground to ward off evil spirits for my sister Maryam. There she was, a tiny woman with an insatiable appetite for rice.

Rice (known as berenj or polo in Farsi) is no afterthought or filler, but the shining star of our family's meals. It comes in countless iterations. It's like that scene from *Forrest Gump* where Bubba goes on and on about shrimp. There's sabzi polo, a forest-green rice laced with herbs, fresh and dried. There's Zereshk Polo (page 144), tart-sweet barberries cascading down a mountain of saffron-laced rice. There's Baghali Polo (page 118) with huge handfuls of dill, Albaloo Polo (page 119) with sour cherries, Loobia Polo (page 122) with a stew of green beans, beef, tomato paste, and cinnamon. Maman made them all masterfully.

On this trip, I came to appreciate the mournful vibes of my previous trips. It's the ancestral weight carried by an ancient people who have been around for many thousands of years and have seen some shit. By comparison, our society, my fellow Americans, is basically a tween. I even turned a corner on taarof after the eighth or ninth Iranian uncle of an uncle, who had seemed so stoic moments before, literally took off his jacket or hat as a gift to us. What I once saw as unhinged hospitality now seemed more like generosity and even responsibility to the culture they inherited.

Edgar brought me to Nixta, but I made it a home (as Persians do), for our guests and for us, with my brand of taarof—a little bit Persian, a little bit Arkansas, a little bit Texas.

DIVAN of

RICE, THE PERSIAN WAY

"My rice doesn't make you topol," Maman would tell my friends, using a Farsi term of endearment that means chubby. She was reassuring me and my fellow insecure thirteen-year-old-mushroom-haircut buds not to worry, she had washed all the "bad starches" out. This was great news (albeit a bald-faced lie). It meant we could eat as much as we wanted of her berenj, each grain distinct and airy, more like a heap of down feathers than a pot of rice.

Topol or not, I've always been a rice girl and later became dead-set on learning her technique. Just about every rice recipe in this book requires a particular soaking, rinsing, and parcooking, so to spare you the repetition and to give them a little love, you'll find the steps here. They seem onerous, but once you get the hang and experience the result, you'll understand why we do it.

1) Put the rice in a bowl and pour in enough water to cover by 1 inch. Stir in enough salt so the water tastes even more intense than ocean water (3 tablespoons of Morton salt for every 3½ cups of water). Let the rice soak in a cool place for at least 2 hours or up to 12 hours (the longer the better).

2) Drain in a fine-mesh sieve, then rinse the rice under cold water, stirring with your fingers, until the water that drains off runs clear, about 2 minutes.

3) In a large pot (nonstick, if you're Maman, but if not, it's not a dealbreaker), bring plenty of water (4 quarts, at least) to a boil over high heat. Maman doesn't salt this water, but many folks do—if you want your rice more seasoned, salt it like ocean water. Add the rice a handful at a time. Boil, stirring occasionally, until the outsides of the grains have softened slightly but the interior is still crunchy, 5 to 6 minutes.

4) Drain the rice in a fine-mesh sieve again and, particularly gently this time, rinse the rice under cold water, stirring with your fingers, until the rice has cooled and the water that drains off runs clear. Give it a good shake to drain well.

WRAP THAT LID

Persians wrap the lids of our rice pots for two reasons. One, the cloth wrapping absorbs steam, so it doesn't condense back into water on the bottom of the lid and drip onto the rice, diminishing that fluff factor. Two, merely draping a towel on the pot is a freaking fire hazard, people.

Here's how to wrap right: Find yourself a nice large, clean kitchen towel (or paper towels) and lay on a work surface. Set your pot's lid on top and gather the edges around the lid, tying or bunching so it stays put.

HOT TIP, THOUGH: You can even buy a lil' floral bonnet—known in Farsi as a damkesh or damkoni—made for this very purpose. Think a shower cap but for the lid of your rice pot.

TAHDIG

Persian rice is famed for its fluffiness and for the tahdig, the coveted crisp, golden layer that develops at the bottom (tah) of the pot (dig) as the rice cooks.

Not every pot of rice has tahdig. But you can tahdig any rice dish you want. At least, according to Maman. And the tahdig isn't always a crispy layer of rice. In Loobia Polo (page 122), a bed of potatoes is tahdig. Whipped up by bouts of creative tahdiggery, Maman has even been known to lay down some sliced cabbage or whole (not broken up) flour tortillas and let them get all crispy.

So, once you get the hang of Persian rice making, get creative! Get that oil going, lay down your delicious flooring, and give it a pat so it makes maximum contact with the hot surface of the pot. Wait a few minutes before spooning in your hill of rice—soaked, parcooked, and all that (see Rice, the Persian Way)—and making your holes, to let the steam escape and encourage the crisping. When your rice is done, peek at the edges on the bottom of the pan and see what's popping off. If the tahdig isn't as browned and crisp as you'd like it, wait a few minutes longer. If it's still not there, scoop out the rice, leaving the tahdig and letting it cook until it's to your liking.

When Maman's in the mood, she'll take tahdig to the next level. Before she adds the first layer of rice, she'll take the grains (about 1 cup) and mix it in a bowl with ½ cup yogurt and 2 egg yolks. Then she spreads the mixture onto the hot surface. As a result, the tahdig holds together in a sultry deeeep brown slab.

In Maman's family, they skip the much ballyhooed pot-flip flourish that neatly deposits the rice onto a platter, tahdig to the sky. Instead, only after the fluffy grains are safely scooped is the tahdig chiseled from the bottom of the pot and either perched on top or served alongside.

RICE IS JUST RICE, RIGHT?

I've never seen Maman more upset than the day she purchased organic rice from a certain upscale market. At every stage in the cooking process, she was furiously muttering to herself about her folly, at her betrayal of her fierce loyalty to Royal brand basmati. Don't worry, she called to inform the store of the mushy rice and embarrassment suffered, and to ask for a refund. LeBron should not have to play with a deflated ball.

Point is, don't be seduced by trust-fund grains or other rices that think they're better than you. Royal is easy enough to get. (Edgar loves it, too, particularly the one that says "Chef's Secret" on the package, which contains extra long grains.) But whatever you choose, get to know it and stick with it. That might've been Maman's true folly. When you make friends with an ingredient, keep her close.

SHIT MAMAN DOES

For most of y'all, Mexican food needs no introduction, but Persian food just might. Like Mexico, Iran is also a vast country with regional cuisines galore. So it's not served well by sweeping generalizations. Yet through observing Maman for the past thirty-seven years and comparing her to other Iranian cooks, I have noticed some qualities that strike me as rather Persian. For ex:

SO MANY ONIONS: The foundation of so many dishes is fried onions and turmeric. That's why, growing up, my clothes always smelled like onions, though somehow Maman, the one frying the onions, always smelled like flowers.

HERBS BY THE FISTFUL: You know how French stews might be sprinkled and Italian sauces green-flecked? Well, a medium-size pot of ghormeh sabzi, the iconic Iranian beef stew, straight up contains a full *dozen bunches* of herbs—of cilantro and scallions and parsley. Kuku sabzi (sabzi means herbs in Farsi) is a cool seven bunches of those same herbs, plus a lil' dill and fenugreek leaves, bound together by four eggs—the proportions of a Euro frittata flipped. Maman would spend a solid day every two weeks washing, drying, and chopping herbs to freeze for her culinary endeavors.

EVEN MORE HERBS: Not just that, we have the audacity to serve alongside these herb-engorged dishes . . . mountains of more herbs that we shovel in our gobs by the fistful between bites. So serve the Persian food in this chapter with sprigs of cilantro, mint leaves, and basil—the citrusy, sweet, especially fragrant Persian variety of basil if you can find it, or the similarly complex Thai basil if you can't . . . and regular old basil if you can only get that.

BE SO HIGH-LOW: Season extravagantly with the finest Iranian saffron while insisting on $12 pots and pans. Be so chaotically thrifty—practically every spice or dried herb in Maman's pantry is in a container that once contained a different spice or herb; if you want the dried mint, look for the jar labeled "lemon pepper."

BE SO SECRETIVE: Toss an extra few garlic cloves into a pot while it bubbles, even though it's just you and your daughter in the kitchen.

THE RICE SOMMELIER: You'll almost always find a rice dish among the plates crowding Maman's table. And while, really, any one goes well with any thing, Maman understands the art of matching the rice with the dishes. Here are her suggested pairings.

Maman's Saffron Rice (page 117): Ghormeh Sabzi (page 156), Khoresht Bademjoon (page 151), Khoresht Karafs (page 148), Baba's Kabob (page 147), Khoresht Gheymeh (page 152), and Fesenjoon (page 159)

Loobia Polo (page 122): Solo, on its own

Baghali Polo (page 118): Mahiche (page 160) and Kuku Sabzi ba Mahi (page 143)

Zereshk Polo ba Morgh (page 144): Solo, on its own

Albaloo Polo (page 119): the chicken stew/portion of Zereshk Polo ba Morgh (page 144)

Tachin (page 127): Solo, on its own

MAMAN'S SAFFRON RICE

The OG

Maman has a whole-ass rainbow of rice dishes in her back pocket. Yet saffron rice is her signature. It's where her skills at rice cookery are on full display. Because it's so simple, the cook cannot hide behind razzle-dazzle like herbs or beef or barberries. Some sneak in yogurt or butter for richness or to double down on the tahdig (the crunchy rice at the bottom of the pot), but Maman's is typically nothing more than rice imbued with the perfume of saffron. Each pot is a kingdom of perfect, fluffy, distinct grains tinted gold by Maman, queen of the stove.

- 2 cups basmati rice, preferably "extra long grain"
- About 3 tablespoons Morton kosher salt
- 4 tablespoons neutral oil, such as grapeseed or canola
- ¼ cup plus 1 teaspoon Saffron Water (it's easy—see page 19)

Serves 4

Following the directions in Rice, the Persian Way (page 112), soak the rice (using the salt listed here), parcook, drain, and rinse.

Rinse and wipe out the large pot you used to parcook the rice. Add 3 tablespoons of the oil, set over medium-high heat, and let the oil just begin to smoke. Sprinkle in just enough rice to cover the bottom of the pot in a more or less single layer and give it a little pat with a wooden spoon. Sprinkle on 1 teaspoon of the saffron water. Wait a few minutes to get the tahdig started.

Next, add the remaining rice a handful at a time and sculpt it into a gently sloping hill. Use a wooden spoon to tenderly nudge any rice that inevitably tumbles off the sides to maintain the hill. (Can you just dump in the rice and sculpt it into a hill? Sure, but Maman would never.)

Using the handle of the wooden spoon, make two holes near the center of the mound that are about 1 inch in diameter and stop at the tahdig. Starting about 1 inch from the edge of the pot, make four more similar holes at 12 o'clock, 3 o'clock, 6 o'clock, and 9 o'clock.

Drizzle the remaining 1 tablespoon oil evenly over the rice.

Wrap the pot's lid with a clean kitchen towel (see how on page 112), cover the pot, and cook over medium-high heat for 10 minutes. Turn the heat to very low (you may want to switch burners to find the one that provides the lowest heat) and cook, covered and without peeking, until the rice is fully tender and the grains on the top are fluffy and distinct from one another, about 30 minutes. If it's not quite done, cover and keep cooking for up to 15 minutes more.

When the rice is done, open the lid, evenly pour on the remaining ¼ cup saffron water, and use a wooden spoon to very gently toss the rice until it turns an even golden color. Scoop the rice onto a serving plate, leaving the tahdig to cook a little more until it's as browned and crispy as you like, up to 10 minutes more.

Use a large spoon to dislodge the tahdig and serve it with the rice. (Keeps in the fridge for up to 5 days.)

BAGHALI POLO

Fava Bean 'n' Dill Rice

A stunning forest green–flecked rice, baghali polo flaunts more fresh favas than an Italian restaurant in springtime and more dill than, I don't know, a dill factory or something. It's delicious beside fish or braised lamb shanks (see page 160). You'll find a pretty picture of those shanks on that rice on page 161.

1¼ cups basmati rice, preferably "extra long grain"
About 3 tablespoons Morton kosher salt
Heaping 1 cup finely chopped dill
¾ cup shelled peeled fava beans or lima beans, fresh or frozen
4 tablespoons neutral oil, such as grapeseed or canola

Serves 4

Following the directions in Rice, the Persian Way (page 112), soak the rice (using the salt listed here) and drain, but don't parcook it just yet.

In a 5- to 6-quart nonstick pot, bring 16 cups water to a boil over high heat, then add the soaked rice, dill, and fava beans a handful at a time. Boil, stirring occasionally, until the outside of the grains have softened slightly but the interior is still crunchy, 4 to 5 minutes. Drain the mixture in a fine-mesh sieve and, particularly gently, rinse under cold water, stirring with your fingers, until the rice has cooled and the water that drains off runs clear. Give it a good shake to drain well.

Rinse and wipe out the pot. Add 3 tablespoons of the oil, set the pot over medium-high heat, and let the oil just begin to smoke. Sprinkle in just enough rice to cover the bottom of the pot in a more or less single layer and give it a little pat with a wooden spoon. Wait a few minutes to get the tahdig started.

Next, add the remaining rice a handful at a time and sculpt it into a gently sloping hill. Use a wooden spoon to tenderly nudge any rice that inevitably tumbles off the sides to maintain the hill. (Can you just dump in the rice and sculpt it into a hill? Sure, but Maman would never.)

Using the handle of the wooden spoon, make two holes in the center of the mound that are about 1 inch in diameter and stop at the tahdig. Starting about 1 inch from the edge of the pot, make four more similar holes at 12 o'clock, 3 o'clock, 6 o'clock, and 9 o'clock. Drizzle the remaining 1 tablespoon oil evenly over the rice.

Wrap the pot's lid with a clean kitchen towel (see how on page 112), cover the pot, and cook over medium-high heat for 10 minutes. Turn the heat to very low (you may want to switch burners to find the one that provides the lowest heat) and cook, covered and without peeking, until the rice is fully tender and the grains on the top are fluffy and distinct from one another, about 30 minutes. If it's not quite done, cover and keep cooking for up to 15 minutes more.

Scoop the rice onto a serving plate, leaving the tahdig to cook a little more until it's as browned and crispy as you like, up to 10 minutes more. Use a large spoon to dislodge the tahdig and serve it with the rice. (Keeps in the fridge for up to 5 days.)

ALBALOO POLO

Cherry Rice

To paraphrase Prince, purple rice, purple riiiiice. The sour cherries, cooked with a lot of sugar and a little butter, are what tint these grains magenta, and the whole thing is studded with baby meatballs. Now that's worth singing about.

RICE

- 2 cups basmati rice, preferably "extra long grain"
- About 3 tablespoons Morton kosher salt

CHERRIES

- 1 pound fresh sour cherries, pitted
- 1⅓ cups sugar
- 1½ tablespoons unsalted butter

MEATBALLS

- 1 medium yellow onion, peeled
- 12 ounces ground beef, preferably 80/20
- ⅓ teaspoon Morton kosher salt
- ⅓ teaspoon freshly ground black pepper
- ⅓ teaspoon ground turmeric
- 4 tablespoons neutral oil, such as grapeseed or canola

ASSEMBLY

- 1 tablespoon neutral oil, such as grapeseed or canola

Serves 4

PREPARE THE RICE: Following the directions in Rice, the Persian Way (page 112), soak the rice (using the salt listed here), parcook, drain, and rinse. Clean the pot and save it for cooking the meatballs.

COOK THE CHERRIES: In a small pot, combine the cherries and sugar and bring to a simmer over medium heat. Cook, stirring occasionally, until the cherries are soft but still hold their shape and the juices that come out have thickened slightly, 15 to 20 minutes.

Remove from the heat and stir in the butter. Drain the cherries in a fine-mesh sieve set over a bowl, reserving the liquid. Set both aside.

MAKE THE MEATBALLS: Grate the onion on the large holes of a box grater directly onto a kitchen towel. Gather the edges, hold it over the sink, and squeeze out as much liquid as you can. In a medium mixing bowl, combine the onion, beef, salt, pepper, and turmeric and mix to distribute the ingredients well, about 2 minutes. Use damp hands to form 1-inch meatballs and transfer to a tray or plate.

In the cleaned nonstick pot, heat the oil over medium until shimmering. Working in batches to avoid overcrowding, cook the meatballs, turning occasionally, until browned all over, about 4 minutes per batch. Transfer them to a tray or plate as they're fried, leaving the fat behind. Set aside.

ASSEMBLE THE DISH: Pour out all but 3 tablespoons of fat from the pot, set over medium-high heat, and let the oil just begin to smoke. Sprinkle in just enough rice to cover the bottom of the pot in a more or less single layer and give it a little pat with a wooden spoon. Wait a few minutes to get the tahdig started.

Next, add an even ½-inch-ish layer of the rice, then a layer of cherries, then a layer of meatballs. Repeat the layering two more times, using smaller layers each time and finishing with a final layer of rice. Sculpt it into a gently sloping hill. Use a wooden spoon to tenderly nudge any rice that inevitably tumbles off the sides to maintain the hill.

CONTINUED

Using the handle of the wooden spoon, make two holes in the center of the mound that are about 1 inch in diameter and stop at the tahdig. Starting about 1 inch from the edge of the pot, make four more similar holes at 12 o'clock, 3 o'clock, 6 o'clock, and 9 o'clock. Drizzle the oil evenly over the rice.

Wrap the pot's lid with a clean kitchen towel (see how on page 112), cover the pot, and cook over medium-high heat for 10 minutes. Turn the heat to very low (you may want to switch burners to find the one that provides the lowest heat) and cook, covered and without peeking, until the rice is fully tender and the grains on the top are fluffy and distinct from one another, about 30 minutes. If it's not quite done, cover and keep cooking for up to 15 minutes more.

When the rice is done, open the lid, evenly pour on some of the reserved cherry cooking liquid, and use a wooden spoon to very gently toss the rice (more liquid = more purple). Scoop the rice onto a serving plate, leaving the tahdig to cook a little more until it's as browned and crispy as you like, up to 10 minutes more.

Use a large spoon to dislodge the tahdig and serve it with the rice. (Keeps in the fridge for up to 3 days.)

LOOBIA POLO

Green Bean 'n' Beef Rice

Some Persian rice steals the show from the stews they're served with. This one *is* the show. The parcooked grains are layered with beef or lamb simmered with loobia (aka green beans), tomato paste, and turmeric; scented with saffron and cinnamon; and steamed to a gorgeous orange-hued jumble. Mast-o-khiar (cucumber yogurt, see Note, page 124) on the side is a must, if you ask me.

STEW

1 pound green beans, trimmed and cut into 1-inch pieces
2½ tablespoons neutral oil, such as grapeseed or canola
1 cup diced red onion
½ teaspoon ground turmeric
½ teaspoon freshly ground black pepper
8 ounces beef chuck, cut into 1-inch cubes
2½ tablespoons unsalted butter
6 tablespoons tomato paste
Hot water, as needed
2 teaspoons Morton kosher salt

ASSEMBLY

2 cups basmati rice, preferably "extra long grain"
About 3 tablespoons Morton kosher salt
6 tablespoons neutral oil, such as grapeseed or canola
2 small red potatoes (6 ounces total), peeled and cut into ¼-inch rounds
6 tablespoons Saffron Water (it's easy—see page 19)
1 teaspoon ground cinnamon
1 tablespoon hot water

Serves 4 to 6

MAKE THE STEW: Set a large skillet over medium-high heat for a minute. Add the beans and 1½ tablespoons of the oil, lower the heat to medium, and cook, stirring occasionally, until tender but crunchy and still bright green, about 10 minutes. Transfer to a plate and set aside.

Add the onion to the skillet and remaining 1 tablespoon oil and cook over medium-high heat until they sizzle. Lower the heat to medium and cook, stirring occasionally, until translucent, about 5 minutes.

Add the turmeric and pepper and cook for 1 minute, then add the beef and stir to coat in the flavorful business. Add the butter and let it melt and bubble. Make a little spot in the skillet, add the tomato paste, and cook, stirring frequently, until it turns a shade darker, about 5 minutes. Stir everything together and cook until the beef is lightly browned, about 10 minutes.

Stir in the green beans. Add enough hot water (about 2 cups) to just cover the ingredients and let it come to a boil over high heat. Cover the skillet (leave a tiny opening for steam to escape) and lower the heat to cook at a steady simmer, stirring occasionally, until the meat is spoon-tender, the beans are silky soft, and almost all the liquid has evaporated, 30 to 35 minutes. Stir in the salt or more to taste.

ASSEMBLE THE DISH: Following the directions in Rice, the Persian Way (page 112), soak the rice (using the salt listed here), parcook, drain, and rinse.

Heat 3 tablespoons of the oil in a 4- to 5-quart pot over high until it shimmers. Add the potatoes in a single layer and cook until they begin to brown, about 5 minutes. Lower the heat to medium-high. Add an even ½-inch-ish layer of the rice, all of the stew, the saffron water, and cinnamon. Finish with the remaining rice and sculpt it into a gently sloping hill.

Drizzle the remaining 3 tablespoons oil over the rice.

CONTINUED

Using the handle of a wooden spoon, make one hole in the center of the mound that's about 1 inch in diameter and stop at the tahdig. Starting about 1 inch from the edge of the pot, make four more similar holes at 12 o'clock, 3 o'clock, 6 o'clock, and 9 o'clock. Drizzle the hot water evenly over the top.

Wrap the pot's lid with a clean kitchen towel (see how on page 112), cover the pot, and cook over medium-high heat for 10 minutes. Turn the heat to very low (you may want to switch burners to find the one that provides the lowest heat) and cook, covered and without peeking, until the rice is fully tender and the grains on the top are fluffy and distinct from one another, about 30 minutes. If it's not quite done, cover and keep cooking for up to 15 minutes more.

Scoop into a serving bowl, leaving the potatoes behind, and mix well so no grains of rice are still white. Keep cooking the potatoes until they're as browned and crispy as you like, up to 10 minutes more.

Use a spatula to remove the crispy potatoes and transfer, browned-side up, to a separate serving plate. (Keeps in the fridge for up to 3 days.)

NOTE: To make mast-o-khiar, mix 2 cups Agha Reza's Mast (page 169) or some nice tangy plain yogurt with 1 or 2 diced Persian (mini) cucumbers, plus a big pinch of salt and dried mint.

NOON BARBARI

Flatbread

She's thicc for flatbread and that's just how we like her. In Iranian bakeries, soft, super-chewy barbari, with their lovely crust and sesame seed sprinkle, are the size of boogie boards. Ours are sized for home vibes, easier to handle and just as tasty. Shout-outs to the indigenous Barbars of Northeastern Iran for this one.

Equipment: stand mixer or handheld mixer

2 cups whole wheat flour
1¾ cups all-purpose flour
2½ teaspoons Morton kosher salt
1 teaspoon sugar
One ¼-ounce packet instant yeast (2¼ teaspoons)
1¾ cups cool water
1½ tablespoons extra-virgin olive oil

TOPPING

4½ tablespoons all-purpose flour
½ cup cool water
2 tablespoons sesame seeds

Makes 2 barbari (serves 8 to 10)

In a stand mixer fitted with the whisk (or in a large bowl with a handheld mixer), mix together the whole wheat flour, all-purpose flour, salt, sugar, and yeast and stir well. Add the cool water and mix on medium speed for about 5 minutes, just to get the ingredients real friendly with one another. Add the olive oil and mix on medium until fully incorporated, about 2 minutes.

Cover the bowl with a towel and let it sit for 30 minutes at room temperature, until it has doubled in size. Then refrigerate, covered, for 8 to 12 hours.

Remove from the fridge and leave it, covered, at room temp for 2 hours. Transfer the dough to a cutting board, cut it into 2 equal portions, then re-cover and let sit for 10 minutes.

Line a large sheet pan with parchment paper. Transfer the dough to the sheet pan and use your fingers to spread and stretch each piece of dough to a rough 12 by 6-inch rectangle that's about ½ inch thick. Starting about 1 inch from a long edge, use your fingertips and a gentle prodding motion to make a nice, deep indented line the long way. Repeat to make 5 or 6 parallel lines every inch or so. Cover and let it rest (last time, I swear) for 30 minutes at room temp.

MEANWHILE, MAKE THE TOPPING: In a small saucepan, combine the flour and cool water and stir well. Bring to a gentle simmer over medium heat and cook, stirring occasionally, for 1 to 2 minutes, until it's the texture of loose yogurt. Set the topping aside.

Preheat the oven to 475°F.

Brush the bread with a layer of the topping and sprinkle on the sesame seeds. Bake until golden brown and crispy on the outside and chewy on the inside, 20 to 25 minutes, rotating the pan halfway through.

Let cool completely before serving. (Keeps in airtight containers at room temp for up to 2 days or in the freezer for up to 3 months. Briefly thaw, if frozen. Toast either way.)

TACHIN

Savory Birthday Cake Rice 'n' Chicken

Birthday cake is fine, but I'd rather stick candles in tachin. Think of a gorgeous savory cake of rice mixed with yogurt and egg that, unlike the Fluffy McFlufferson rice dishes we highlight elsewhere, is dense but still somehow not heavy. Flavored with aromatic saffron and topped with tart zereshk (barberries), this banger is baked until it develops a crunchy, deep golden crust that's better than any icing. Is it cake? Is it rice? It's both!

CHICKEN

- 2 pounds boneless, skinless chicken breasts
- 1 small yellow onion, thinly sliced
- 1 tablespoon Morton kosher salt
- 1½ teaspoons freshly ground black pepper
- 1½ teaspoons ground turmeric
- 1½ teaspoons Saffron Water (it's easy—see page 19)
- 2 tablespoons neutral oil, such as grapeseed or canola, plus more if necessary

ASSEMBLY

- 3 cups basmati rice, preferably "extra long grain"
- Morton kosher salt
- 1 egg
- 4 egg yolks
- 1 cup yogurt, store-bought or homemade (see page 169), plus more for serving
- 3 tablespoons rose water
- 1 tablespoon Saffron Water (it's easy—see page 19)
- 1 tablespoon neutral oil, such as grapeseed or canola, plus more for the pan
- ½ cup Zereshk (page 170), for serving
- Chopped unsalted roasted pistachios, for serving

Serves 4 to 6

COOK THE CHICKEN: In a large bowl, combine the chicken, onion, salt, pepper, turmeric, and saffron water and mix really well.

Heat the oil in a large skillet over medium-high until it shimmers. Working in batches and adding another splash of oil if necessary, cook the chicken mixture, flipping occasionally, until lightly browned and cooked through, 10 to 15 minutes. Set aside to cool, and shred the chicken.

ASSEMBLE THE DISH: Following the directions in Rice, the Persian Way (page 112), soak the rice (using 3 tablespoons of salt), parcook, drain, and rinse.

Preheat the oven to 400°F.

In a large bowl, combine the whole egg, egg yolks, yogurt, rose water, saffron water, the 1 tablespoon oil, and 1 teaspoon of salt and whisk until smooth. About one-quarter at a time, add the rinsed rice, gently mixing so it's all evenly coated in the yogurt business.

Grease the bottom and sides of a heavy 9 by 13-inch baking dish with oil. Spoon in half the rice mixture and spread to an even layer. Add the chicken and onions in an even layer, then top with a layer of the remaining rice. Use your hand (at least, if you want Maman's approval) to give the top layer of rice a gentle press to squish it against the chicken.

Cover tightly with foil and use a small knife to poke 8 to 10 small slits in the foil. Bake until deep golden and slightly crispy at the edges, 1 to 1½ hours, rotating the pan halfway through.

Run a knife along the edges to loosen the tachin, then carefully invert it onto a serving platter. Spoon on the zereshk and pistachios and serve hot or room temp with a bowl of yogurt on the side.

AMEH FOUROUZ'S MORABA HAVIJ

Carrot Jam

My ameh (aunt) Fourouz is neck and neck with Maman in the race for Persian cooking GOAT. Her carrot jam, for instance, is the jam. She almost always has some in the fridge. When you come over, she'll grab some bread, like barbari (page 125), spread on a little soft butter, then slather it with her moraba havij (that's Farsi for carrot jam). It is the ultimate loghmeh—the bite that a loved one makes you and shoves into your mouth as a snack. It's sweet, but not too sweet, the earthiness of the carrots and the warmth of the cardamom giving it a savory edge, and the rose water and saffron making it super aromatic. Like I said, it's the jam.

Edgar knows some shit about jam, and he says it's the best he's ever had. Ameh sent him the recipe in a text punctuated with emojis, so we could serve it at Nixta. We used black carrots we found at the market to make a neo-goth version, a jam that just don't give a fuck. Goth or not, it goes great on any bread (especially barbari) with either cream cheese, butter, or whipped ricotta. Some roughly chopped pistachios on there, that's classic. I like it with some hot Lahijan tea.

1 pound trimmed carrots
1⅔ cups sugar
1¼ cups water
8 cardamom pods, preferably black
2 tablespoons rose water
1 teaspoon Saffron Water (it's easy—see page 19)

Makes about 1¾ cups

Peel the carrots or don't—the skin is a-okay as long as you wash them well. Grate them on the large holes of a box grater.

In a medium pot, combine the carrots, sugar, water, and cardamom. Bring the mixture to a boil, then lower the heat and simmer gently, stirring occasionally (but more frequently near the end), until the liquid is syrupy and the carrots are glossy and tender but not mushy, about 1 hour.

Add the rose water and saffron water and give the whole thing another few minutes of simmering, just to let it all meld. Turn off the heat and let it cool completely. (Keeps in the fridge for up to 2 months. Eat around the cardamom pods.)

NOTE: Though you can totally eyeball it, we like to use the "plate test" to tell when the jam is properly jammified. While it's simmering, stick a small plate in the freezer for 10 minutes. When you want to check if it's done, add a small spoonful of jam to the plate, let it cool for a minute, then poke it with your finger. Does it still run like syrup? Keep simmering. Does it look set like jam? Nice! Move on to the next step.

OMELETTE IROONI

Tomato 'n' Eggs

No, for the ten millionth time, this is not shakshuka. I mean, same vibes and probably cousins, but this is the simple but spectacular tomatoey egg situation that was typically on Maman's breakfast table. It's great on crusty bread or tucked into warm tortillas or accompanied by the full Persian spread: Noon Barbari (page 125), walnuts, feta, lots of herbs, Shoori (page 171), and maybe some carrot jam (page 128). Coffee works, but Lahijan tea is the move.

- 2 tablespoons neutral oil, such as grapeseed or canola
- 1 medium yellow onion, thinly sliced
- ½ teaspoon ground turmeric
- ½ teaspoon freshly ground black pepper
- 2¼ pounds Roma or plum tomatoes, cut into ½-inch dice
- 1½ teaspoons Morton kosher salt, or more to taste
- 5 eggs
- Mixed herbs (cilantro, mint leaves, and/or Persian or Thai basil), for serving

Serves 2 to 3

Heat the oil in a large nonstick skillet over medium-high until it shimmers. Add the onion and cook, stirring occasionally, until browned at the edges, 4 to 6 minutes.

Stir in the turmeric and pepper and cook for a minute to bring out the aromas. Add the tomatoes, let them get juicy, and then let that liquid tighten up a bit so it's saucy not soupy, about 10 minutes. Stir in the salt.

Lower the heat to medium, crack the eggs into the sauce with some space between them, and cook, stirring just the edges of the whites to incorporate them with some of the sauce, for 5 minutes. Cover and continue cooking until the whites are set and the yolks runny, 3 to 4 minutes more.

Season with salt to taste and serve right away with the mixed herbs.

HALIM BADEMJOON

Eggplant 'n' Beef Porridge

One day in Bandar Abbas, a port in the south of Iran, Edgar and I stumbled upon a gigantic bubbling pot, right there on the street. I swear Edgar went up and stuck his whole head in to see if it passed the ol' Sniff-N-Sizzle Test—if something smells good *and* it's making cooking noises, you should get you some. The presiding mustachioed gentlemen spooned us bowls and we ate the version of the halim you see here, flavorful braised beef or lamb mashed with rice and eggplant to a glorious porridge and then seasoned with the umami-bomb-y fermented yogurt called kashk.

- 1¾ pounds beef or lamb neck slices
- 2 medium yellow onions, 1 quartered, 1 thinly sliced
- 1 tablespoon freshly ground black pepper
- 1 tablespoon ground turmeric
- 1 tablespoon advieh (Persian spice blend, see Note)
- 3½ tablespoons Morton kosher salt
- 1 cup basmati rice, preferably "extra long grain"
- 1¾ pounds Japanese eggplants (about 8) or Chinese eggplants (about 4), tops removed and peeled
- About ½ cup neutral oil, such as grapeseed or canola
- 2 teaspoons dried mint
- 4 garlic cloves, roughly chopped
- ½ cup finely chopped walnuts
- ½ cup liquid kashk, plus more to taste
- 4 teaspoons Nana Dagh (page 170), for serving
- Noon Barbari (optional; page 125), for serving
- Mixed herbs (cilantro, mint leaves, and/or Persian or Thai basil), for serving

Serves 4

NOTE: Maman gets down with fragrant advieh, a mix of spices like cumin, cardamom, and dried rose petals, that you can buy online or in stores with a Persian bent. And you *should*, too.

In a medium pot, combine the beef, quartered onion, pepper, turmeric, advieh, and enough water to cover by 1 inch. Bring to a boil, cover, and lower the heat to cook at a gentle simmer until very tender, about 2 hours. Transfer the beef to a bowl and shred the meat, discarding the bones. Set the cooking liquid aside.

Meanwhile, in a small pot, bring 3 cups water to a boil and stir in 2½ tablespoons of the salt, add the rice, and cook, stirring occasionally, until al dente, about 6 minutes. Drain in a fine-mesh sieve and briefly rinse under cold water. Set aside.

Halve the eggplants lengthwise. If they're long boys, cut them crosswise, too. Toss the eggplants with 1½ teaspoons of the salt and let them hang out for 25 minutes to draw out liquid. Pat dry with paper towels.

Heat a large skillet over medium-high for a minute or so. Working in two or three batches, cook the eggplants, drizzling on 2 tablespoons of oil per batch and turning occasionally, until soft and deep golden brown all over, 8 to 10 minutes per batch. Transfer to a cutting board and roughly chop.

Heat another 2 tablespoons oil in the same skillet over medium-high until it shimmers. Add the sliced onion and cook, stirring, until browned at the edges, 4 to 6 minutes. (If you want, reserve some for serving.)

Off the heat, add the dried mint and garlic and stir for 2 minutes. Back on medium-high, add the shredded beef, ½ cup of the reserved beef cooking liquid, the eggplant, and remaining 1½ teaspoons salt. Spend a few minutes mashing everything with a blunt object, like the wooden mallet thingie that exists only in Persian households or more likely a potato masher.

Adjust the heat to medium-low, then add the rice and mix for 1 minute. Stir in the walnuts, cover, and cook until the rice is fully cooked, about 10 minutes.

Uncover and cook for 15 minutes more, bashing and mixing every 5 minutes, until you have a coarse mash. Stir in the kashk and ¾ cup of the reserved beef cooking liquid (save the rest for something, because it's tasty) and cook for 10 minutes to meld the flavors. Season with more kashk to taste.

Serve in bowls topped with the reserved fried onions and a drizzle of the nana dagh. Eat with barbari and herbs.

MIRZA GHASEMI

Eggplant 'n' Hella Garlic Dip

Garlic lovers assemble! While mirza ghasemi is technically a side dish/dip situation, a lot of Iranians (especially near the Caspian Sea) eat this gloriously garlicky eggplant mash in the morning with a fried egg on top, even though there are already eggs up in there. Eat it with any type of bread—but especially Noon Barbari (page 125)—or rice on the side. A pile of herbs would be bomb, too.

Using a broiler and vegetable oil is just fine, but enlisting a charcoal grill to cook the eggplant and beef tallow to cook the dip give it another layer of smokiness and umami.

Equipment: charcoal grill, charcoal, ½ cup hickory chips

3 Chinese eggplants (about 1¼ pounds total)
1 pound tomatoes, whole
½ cup beef tallow or vegetable oil
12 garlic cloves, thinly sliced
3 tablespoons tomato paste
1 teaspoon ground turmeric
¾ teaspoon Morton kosher salt
1 tablespoon unsalted butter
4 eggs, lightly beaten
Noon Barbari (page 125) or rice, for serving
Mixed herbs (cilantro, mint leaves, and/or Persian or Thai basil), for serving
Fried eggs, for serving

Serves 4 to 6

Prepare a charcoal grill to cook with indirect heat—you know, hot stuff goes on one side, eggplants on the other.

Sprinkle the hickory chips evenly onto the coals. Add the eggplant to the opposite side of the grill, cover, and cook, flipping occasionally, until very soft, about 45 minutes. (Alternatively, you can broil them, flipping occasionally, until charred all over and very soft, about 40 minutes.)

Set aside until cool enough to handle, then remove and discard the peel and top thingie. Roughly chop the soft flesh, then pop it into a sieve set over a bowl and set aside to drain until you add it later.

Bring a medium pot of water to a boil. Cut a little shallow "X" through the skin on the bottom of the tomatoes, then give them like 30 seconds in the boiling water, just to loosen the skins. Let them cool, then peel, core, and chop them into 1-inch pieces.

In a large nonstick skillet, combine the tallow and garlic. Set over medium heat and cook, stirring, until the garlic is golden brown, about 6 minutes.

Add the tomato paste, turmeric, and salt and cook, stirring, until the tomato paste turns a shade or two darker, about 5 minutes.

Add the eggplant and cook for 5 minutes to bring all those flavors together. Add the tomatoes, put the lid on the pan, and get a steady simmer going, stirring occasionally, for 10 minutes. Stir in the butter, adjust the heat to low, and let it simmer, covered, for another 10 minutes.

Increase the heat back to medium. Add the eggs, stir gently, and cook, stirring occasionally, until the eggs look scrambled, 2 to 3 minutes. Season to taste with salt.

Serve with barbari or rice and herbs. If desired, serve with fried eggs.

SALAD OLOVIEH

Maman's (not Dayee Hamid's) Potato Salad

Potato salad is serious business in my family, so serious it caused an as-yet-irreparable rift between Maman and her brother Hamid. It was the day of my cousin Amir Nader's wedding and the guests had all brought something to the potluck buffet. Maman came through with her version of tangy, delicious Olivier salad ("Olovieh," for us), aka Russian salad. And with horror, she saw it: In prime position as the first of the buffet offerings and laden with chopped hot dog and bologna, Dayee Hamid's Olovieh salad.

She did what any rational Maman would do. She put hers in the first spot and moved his all the way to the end. When confronted, she declared it a simple matter of food safety—his salad, she claimed, had been made a week prior. Hamid felt betrayed. I'm far from impartial, but my guess is that Maman acted out of well-earned pride. She makes her salad with grated potatoes and fluffy egg whites, enlivens it with gherkins and mustard, and bulks it with turmeric-y shredded chicken. It's also blessedly hot dog free.

Perfect for picnics and potlucks, the salad is especially welcome with tortillas or lavash, herbs, Baba's Kabob (page 147), and Shoori (page 171).

- 2¼ pounds Yukon Gold potatoes
- Morton kosher salt
- 1 tablespoon neutral oil, such as grapeseed or canola
- 3 boneless, skinless chicken breasts (about 18 ounces total)
- 1 teaspoon freshly ground black pepper
- 1 teaspoon ground turmeric
- 2 cups drained cornichons, sliced into ¼-inch rounds
- 6 tablespoons Miracle Whip (Team Maman) or Duke's (Team Edgar)
- 6 tablespoons yellow mustard
- 5 hard-boiled eggs (whites only), cut into ¼-inch dice
- Mixed herbs (cilantro, mint leaves, and/or Persian or Thai basil), for serving

Serves 4 to 6

In a medium pot, combine the potatoes, 1 tablespoon kosher salt, and water to cover by 1 inch. Bring to a simmer and cook until tender, 20 to 30 minutes. Drain, let cool, then peel and grate the potatoes on the large holes of a box grater.

Meanwhile, heat the oil in a large skillet over medium-high until it shimmers. Season the chicken breasts all over with the pepper, turmeric, and 2 teaspoons kosher salt and cook, flipping occasionally, until lightly browned and cooked through, 10 to 15 minutes. Set aside to cool, then chop and shred the chicken.

In a large bowl, combine the potatoes, chicken, cornichons, "mayo," mustard, and egg whites and mixy mixy. Season to taste with salt.

Refrigerate for at least 1 hour or (ahem, Dayee Hamid) up to 3 days. Serve with herbs on the side for munching.

SALAD SHIRAZI

The Salad on Every Persian Table

Salad shirazi is a fresh, crisp, bright delight—a staple on the Persian table and throughout the Middle East. At its most basic, it's chopped tomatoes, cukes, and onion lavished with olive oil, citrus, and, as you might guess if you've been paying any attention at all, plenty of fresh-ass herbs. This version shines thanks to tangy sumac and a mix of vegetation that approximates flavors we loved in shirazi salads in Iran.

- 3 tablespoons extra-virgin olive oil
- 2 tablespoons fresh lime juice, plus more to taste
- 1 teaspoon ground sumac
- ½ teaspoon Morton kosher salt, plus more to taste
- ½ teaspoon freshly ground black pepper, plus more to taste
- 12 ounces Persian (mini) cucumbers (about 3), cut into ¼-inch dice
- 10 ounces tomatoes, cut into ¼-inch pieces
- 1 small red onion, cut into ⅛-inch cubes
- 1 cup finely chopped mixed herbs (cilantro, mint leaves, and/or Persian or Thai basil)

Serves 4

In a small bowl, whisk together the olive oil, lime juice, sumac, salt, and pepper until emulsified—you know, well combined and a little creamy.

In a large serving bowl, combine the cucumbers, tomatoes, onion, and herbs and toss gently but well. Pour the dressing over the salad, toss well, and season to taste with more lime, salt, and pepper.

Let the salad hang out to marinate for 10 minutes before serving.

KOTLET

Meat 'n' Potato Patties

Everyone get in the car, we're going to Lavasoon! So, we did. Eight of us stacked in a tiny Peugeot to enjoy the freshwater creeks and waterfalls in this mountain town outside Tehran. And what did we pack, you ask? Kotlet, of course, the perfect Persian picnic food. These little patties of ground minced beef or lamb, mashed potatoes, onion, turmeric, and eggs are breaded and fried to a crisp.

This is perfect with lavash (or flour tortillas, like we did in Arkansas) as well as lots of herbs, raw onions, sliced tomatoes, and shoori (pickled veg). They're also fantastic cold on a hero with those same fixings piled on. Served with ketchup, Edgar, not mayo. Jeez.

1 medium yellow onion, peeled
1¼ pounds Yukon Gold potatoes (about 4 medium), peeled
1 pound ground beef, preferably 80/20
1 egg, lightly beaten
2½ teaspoons Morton kosher salt, plus more for sprinkling
1 tablespoon Saffron Water (it's easy—see page 19)
½ teaspoon ground turmeric
½ teaspoon freshly ground black pepper
⅛ teaspoon red pepper flakes
1½ cups fine bread crumbs (Team Maman) or panko (Team Edgar)
Neutral oil, such as grapeseed or canola, for shallow-frying

FOR SERVING

Lavash or flour tortillas (store-bought tortillas, or homemade; see page 189)
Mixed herbs (cilantro, mint leaves, and/or Persian or Thai basil)
Thinly sliced onions
Sliced tomatoes
Shoori (page 171)

Serves 4 to 6

Grate the onion and potatoes on the large holes of a box grater onto a clean kitchen towel. Gather the edges, hold it over the sink, and twist to squeeze out as much liquid as possible.

Transfer the onion and potatoes to a medium bowl. Add the beef, egg, salt, saffron water, turmeric, pepper, and pepper flakes, then spend a good 3 to 5 minutes kneading and squishing them together. You're combining them well, but this rough mixing gives you that kotlet texture. Set aside at room temp for 30 minutes.

Put the bread crumbs in a shallow bowl. Divide the meat mixture in 12 equal-ish pieces. One by one, shape each into a little oval torpedo (4 to 5 inches long), then add it to the panko, turning and patting to coat. Gently press to flatten to a ½-inch thickness, poke a hole all the way through the center with your index finger, and transfer to a plate. Repeat with the remaining meat mixture. (At this point, you can cover and refrigerate for up to 1 day.)

Line a baking sheet with paper towels and keep them near the stove. Pour ½ inch of oil into a large skillet over medium heat. You know it's ready for cooking when you toss in a test bread crumb and it bubbles right away.

Working in batches to avoid overcrowding, fry the kotlets until deep brown and crispy on both sides, 4 to 5 minutes per side. (The hole is supposed to close up, don't stress.) As they're fried, transfer to the paper towels to drain and lightly sprinkle with salt.

TO SERVE: They're great hot, room temp, or cold. Serve with a bread thing, lots of herbs, onions, tomatoes, and shoori.

AUSH RESHTEH

Thicc Herby Noodle Soup

A soup so thick and hearty that rice is, gasp, unnecessary. After all, this stand-alone dish packs kidney beans and garbanzos, split peas and noodles. A healthy dose of dried mint and a bushel of parsley, cilantro, and scallions keep things fresh. When you serve, don't neglect the drip: crispy onions, aromatic fried mint oil, and the tangy, flavor-enhancing kashk.

SOUP

4 tablespoons canola or vegetable oil
2 medium yellow onions, cut into ¼-inch dice
6 garlic cloves, roughly chopped
1 teaspoon ground turmeric
1 teaspoon freshly ground black pepper
2 tablespoons all-purpose flour
2 tablespoons dried mint
One 15-ounce can chickpeas, drained and rinsed
One 15-ounce can kidney beans, drained and rinsed
1 cup yellow split peas (about 8 ounces)
4 cups baby or mature spinach (4 ounces)
2 cups pretty finely chopped flat-leaf parsley (2 bunches)
1½ cups pretty finely chopped cilantro (1 large bunch)
¾ cup thinly sliced scallions, dark-green tops only (from 2 bunches)
3 cups hot water, plus more as needed
1 tablespoon Morton kosher salt, or more to taste
One 12-ounce package aush reshteh noodles (or linguine), broken in half

FOR SERVING

Store-bought fried shallots or onions (Vietnamese, Thai, or Iranian)
Nana Dagh (page 170)
Liquid kashk
Mixed herbs (cilantro, mint leaves, and/or Persian or Thai basil), for serving

Serves 6 to 8

MAKE THE SOUP: Heat the oil in a large skillet over medium-high until it shimmers. Add the onions and cook, stirring frequently, until browned at the edges, about 10 minutes. Add the garlic and cook, stirring, until golden brown, about 3 minutes.

Add the turmeric and pepper and cook, stirring, for 30 seconds. Add the flour and cook, stirring and scraping the pan, for another 30 seconds. Remove from the heat, add the dried mint, and stir for a minute or so (to keep the mint from burning). Set aside.

In a large pot, bring 8 cups water to a boil. Add the chickpeas, kidney beans, and split peas and let it come back to a boil. Lower the heat to cook at a nice strong simmer, stirring occasionally, until the split peas are tender, 10 to 15 minutes.

Add the spinach, parsley, cilantro, and scallion tops to the pot and cook, stirring occasionally and reducing the heat as needed, for 15 minutes. Add the onion mixture and cook, stirring occasionally, until the soup thickens, about 15 minutes more.

Stir in the hot water and salt and bring to a boil. Add the noodles, cover (leave a tiny opening for steam to escape), and cook, stirring occasionally, until the noodles are cooked the way you like them, 12 to 15 minutes. As necessary, top up with hot water, but keep in mind the soup should be thick. Season to taste with more salt, keeping in mind the kashk you'll add later is salty, too.

TO SERVE: Transfer to bowls, garnish with crispy onions, nana dagh, kashk, and herbs.

NOTE: Make it day of or a night or two before, so the flavors can mingle in the fridge.

MAMAN'S SPAGHETTI

Eminem-Approved

Maman hates cuss words—for her, "shut up" is scandalous—but she loves Eminem. I suspect it's because he mentions "mom's spaghetti." Maman loves spaghetti, which goes by makaroni in Farsi and which she treats a bit like rice. She parcooks it, then layers in some simple saucy beef business—think Persian Bolognese—and cooks the whole thing so the noodles on the bottom of the pan (along with some sliced taters) become irresistibly crunchy tahdig that everyone in my family fights over.

SAUCY BUSINESS

- 3 tablespoons neutral oil, such as grapeseed or canola
- 1 medium white onion, cut into ¼-inch dice
- 1 teaspoon ground turmeric
- 1 teaspoon freshly ground black pepper
- 1½ teaspoons Morton kosher salt, plus more to taste
- 1 pound ground beef, preferably 80/20
- ¼ cup tomato paste
- 1 Roma or plum tomato, cut into ¼-inch dice
- 4 garlic cloves, roughly chopped
- ½ red or orange bell pepper, cut into ¼-inch dice
- 1 cup water

ASSEMBLY

- 2 tablespoons neutral oil, such as grapeseed or canola
- 1 tablespoon Morton kosher salt
- 16 ounces spaghetti
- 2 medium Yukon Gold potatoes, peeled and sliced in ½-inch-thick rounds
- ½ cup water

Serves 4 to 6

MAKE THE SAUCY BUSINESS: Heat the oil in a medium pot over medium-high until it shimmers. Add the onion and cook, stirring occasionally, until browned at the edges, 4 to 6 minutes.

Stir in the turmeric, pepper, and salt and cook for a minute. Add the beef and cook, stirring and breaking up clumps, until cooked through and browned, 5 to 8 minutes.

Stir in the tomato paste and cook until it turns a shade darker, about 5 minutes.

Stir in the tomatoes, garlic, and bell pepper and cook for a minute. Add the water, bring to a simmer, and cook until thickened slightly, about 5 minutes. Season to taste with salt. Transfer to a bowl and clean the pot.

ASSEMBLE THE DISH: Bring water to a boil in the cleaned pot and add 1 tablespoon of the oil and the salt. Break the spaghetti in half (avert your eyes, Italians!) and cook, stirring occasionally, until halfway done, about 5 minutes. Drain the pasta and rinse with warm water. (I said avert!)

Heat the remaining 1 tablespoon oil in a large nonstick sauté pan over medium-high until it shimmers. Add the potatoes in a single layer and cook undisturbed for 4 minutes.

Lower the heat to medium. Add three alternating layers of spaghetti and the sauce. No need to spread out the sauce. To the bowl that had the sauce in it, add the water, give it a little stir, and pour evenly into the sauté pan. Cover and let the liquid bubble, 1 to 2 minutes.

Lower the heat to medium-low and cook, covered, until the spaghetti is tender and the potatoes and spaghetti on the bottom are crunchy, about 25 minutes.

Run a knife along the edges to loosen, then carefully invert the dish onto a serving platter. Serve hot.

KUKU SABZI BA MAHI

Maman's Fish with Herby McHerbison Frittata

Mamans be like, "But I didn't have time to cook," then they bust out the trifecta: perfect mayo-slathered fish with steamy, fabulously fluffy rice and kuku sabzi for a little razz pizzazz.

Kuku is a perfect name for a sassy three-legged wiener dog. It's also the Farsi word for a category of foods bound with egg. Sabzi means herbs, and the dish is a raging herb party—I'm talking giant handfuls of parsley, cilantro, and scallions (plus a pinch of dill and fenugreek leaves) with just enough eggs to hold them all together. The result is a striking green with a crisp exterior—frittata(ish) without the breakfast connotation.

KUKU

- 3 bunches of flat-leaf parsley, all but 1 inch of stems trimmed
- 2 bunches of cilantro, all but 1 inch of stems trimmed
- 2 bunches of scallions, roots trimmed
- 3 tablespoons pickled dill
- 1 tablespoon dried fenugreek leaves (shambalileh)
- 4 eggs
- 2 tablespoons finely chopped garlic, or 1 tablespoon garlic powder
- 1½ teaspoons Morton kosher salt
- 1 tablespoon freshly ground black pepper
- ¼ cup plus 2 tablespoons neutral oil, such as grapeseed or canola

FISH

- 1 tablespoon Miracle Whip (Team Maman) or Duke's (Team Edgar)
- 1 tablespoon yellow mustard
- 1½ teaspoons lemon pepper
- A heaping ¼ teaspoon saffron threads, crushed
- 4 fish fillets (6 to 8 ounces each), either tilapia (Team Maman) or snapper (Team Edgar)
- 2 tablespoons neutral oil, such as grapeseed or canola
- ½ tablespoon unsalted butter

FOR SERVING

- Baghali Polo (page 118)
- Mixed herbs (cilantro, mint leaves, and/or Persian or Thai basil)

Serves 4 to 6

MAKE THE KUKU: Wash and thoroughly dry the parsley, cilantro, scallions, and dill. Chop them by hand (the best way) or give them a quick rough chop then buzz them in a food processor (but don't tell Maman) until they're pretty finely chopped. Add them to a large bowl along with the dried fenugreek leaves.

Lightly beat the eggs in a medium bowl, then add them to the big bowl along with the garlic, salt, and pepper and mix really well.

Heat ¼ cup of the oil in a 10-inch nonstick skillet over medium-high until it smokes lightly. Lower the heat to medium. Stir the egg mixture well, then add it to the skillet. Spread to an even layer, and cook, without messing with it, until the bottom has browned, about 8 minutes. Cover and continue cooking until the surface is set but still soft in the center, 2 to 3 minutes.

Use a spatula to nudge the edges to make sure it releases from the skillet. Quickly and confidently flip the kuku onto a plate.

Heat the remaining 2 tablespoons oil in the pan, still over medium-high, until shimmery. Carefully slide the kuku browned-side up back into the pan to cook the second side, still on medium-high, until the second side has browned, 3 to 5 minutes more.

While the kuku finishes cooking, wipe off the serving plate and line it with a double layer of paper towels. Carefully slide the finished kuku onto the prepared plate. Peel away the paper towels, cut the kuku into pizza-slice wedges, and set aside. (At this point, you can store the kuku for up to 2 hours at room temp or in the fridge for up to 4 days.)

COOK THE FISH: In a small bowl, mix together the mayo, mustard, lemon pepper, and saffron. (If you've got the time, let it hang out for 30 minutes or even an hour—that way the color really pops.) Rub the mixture all over the fish fillets.

Heat the oil and butter in a large nonstick pan over medium-high until the butter melts and the fat shimmers. Working in batches, cook the fish, flipping once, until the fish is lightly browned on both sides and flakes easily at the thickest part, 4 to 6 minutes per batch. If needed, add a little more oil.

TO SERVE: Transfer the fish to plates and serve with a wedge or two of the kuku sabzi, the baghali polo, and herbs.

ZERESHK POLO BA MORGH

Barberry Rice 'n' Chicken Stew

As soon as I land in Arkansas, Maman knows the drill. By the time my sister Maryam picks me up at the airport in her minivan, with J, Willow, and Ren in tow (and Maman has called and texted seven times asking where we are), Maman's kitchen smells like onions, turmeric, and rose water. By the time I pull up to her house, the chicken is tender and the saffron rice is steamy. When I sit down, she scatters barberries, like tart-sweet rubies, onto the rice, like a jewel thief spreading her plunder on the bed after a heist. Nothing tastes more like home.

CHICKEN

- 4 tablespoon neutral oil, such as grapeseed or canola
- 4 whole chicken legs (about 3½ pounds total)
- 1 medium yellow onion, cut into ½-inch dice
- 1 teaspoon Morton kosher salt, plus more to taste
- 1 teaspoon ground turmeric
- 2½ cups water
- 2 tablespoons tomato paste
- 2 tablespoons rose water
- 1 tablespoon fresh lemon juice
- 2 teaspoons Saffron Water (it's easy—see page 19)

FOR SERVING

- Maman's Saffron Rice (page 117)
- Zereshk (page 170)
- Mixed herbs (cilantro, mint leaves, and/or Persian or Thai basil)

Serves 4

COOK THE CHICKEN: Heat 2 tablespoons of the oil in a medium Dutch oven or braiser over medium until it shimmers. Add the chicken, onion, salt, and turmeric and cook, stirring and flipping occasionally, until the chicken and onion are golden brown in spots, about 10 minutes.

Add the water, bring to a boil, then cover and cook at a moderate simmer for 15 minutes.

Heat the remaining 2 tablespoons oil in a small skillet over medium-high until it shimmers. Stir in the tomato paste, then add the rose water, lemon juice, and saffron water and stir constantly for 30 seconds.

Add the tomato mixture to the pot with the chicken, stir well, then cover and simmer for 15 minutes more. Uncover and cook until the chicken is cooked through and tender and the sauce thickens a bit, about 10 minutes. Season to taste with salt.

TO SERVE: Sprinkle the saffron rice with the zereshk. Serve the chicken hot alongside the rice and herbs.

BABA'S KABOB

BBQ Meat on a Stick

If you ask any Persian man, the best kabobs are the ones he makes. If that man himself is on the lookout for kabobs, however, it's the vendor with the dirtiest hands who makes the best. My baba is humble and his fingers are far from filthy, and still his koobideh (a type of kabob made with ground meat) is pretty fire. Baba's kabob is made from a combo of ground beef and lamb, seasoned with little more than onion, salt, and pepper, and then grilled directly over fire. (If you prefer, skip the lamb and use 1 pound 70/30 beef.) Always and forever: Flame-licked tomatoes on the side and lemony, salty sumac (the pulverized dried berries of the *Rhus coriaria* plant) sprinkled on top.

Serve with saffron rice or a thin bread, like lavash or warm flour tortillas, that you can use like an edible oven mitt to pull the meat from the skewers so the bread gets all meat-juiced up.

Equipment: 8 wide flat kabob skewers (25 inches long; see Notes), outdoor grill (preferably charcoal)

KABOBS

- 8 ounces ground lamb, preferably nice and fatty
- 8 ounces ground beef, preferably 80/20
- 1 medium white onion (about 8 ounces), peeled but whole
- 1 medium red onion (about 5 ounces), peeled but whole
- ½ teaspoon baking soda
- 1 teaspoon Morton kosher salt
- 1 teaspoon freshly ground black pepper
- Heaping ½ teaspoon ground turmeric
- 6 Roma or plum tomatoes

FOR SERVING

- Sumac
- Mixed herbs (cilantro, mint leaves, and/or Persian or Thai basil)
- Thinly sliced red onions
- Agha Reza's Mast (page 169) or any good tangy yogurt
- Doogh (page 175)
- Maman's Saffron Rice (page 117)

Serves 6

MAKE THE MEAT MIXTURE: Grab a large bowl, add the lamb and beef, and spend a good 3 to 5 minutes kneading and squishing them together. You're combining them well, but this rough mixing is what makes the meat cling to the skewer later.

Into a medium bowl, grate both of the onions on the large holes of a box grater. Add the baking soda and mix well. Lightly squeeze the onion to release excess juicy stuff into the bowl and discard it. Add the onions to the large bowl along with the salt, pepper, and turmeric and mix really well until it sticks to your hands. Cover and refrigerate for at least 2 hours. (At this point, you can refrigerate the meat mixture for up to 24 hours.)

ASSEMBLE THE KABOBS: Divide the mixture into 6 roughly equal portions and roll them into balls. Use a skewer to impale each ball, moving it down a couple inches from the tip of the skewer, then giving it some tender squeezes in your palm to make a nice meat log 1½ inches thick and 8 inches long. Leave a good couple inches empty on either end of the skewers.

As you make each one, set them somewhere where the sticky-ass meat won't touch anything, like across a large skillet or baking dish. They can hang out in the fridge while you do stuff. Impale the whole tomatoes on the last two skewers.

Remove the grill grates, then prepare the grill (preferably with charcoal) to cook with high heat—with a nice pile of red-hot coals that comes up 4 to 6 inches from the grates.

Rest each end of the skewers on the edges of the grill so the meat and tomatoes cook directly over the coals. Cook the tomatoes, turning occasionally until they're charred and tender, 15 to 20 minutes. Cook the meat skewers, flipping them every 15 seconds, until they're a little charred and well done (don't worry, they'll still be juicy), about 6 minutes.

TO SERVE: Transfer to plates. Sprinkle generously with sumac and serve with the grilled tomatoes, herbs, sliced red onions, mast, doogh, and saffron rice.

NOTES: The kabob skewers should be long enough to rest across your grill—a standard Weber kettle is 22 inches across, so 25-inch skewers would be perfect—but if not, you can jury-rig it, say, by balancing their ends on some bricks.

KHORESHT KARAFS

Celery 'n' Beef Stew

Cooked celery is usually a backup dancer, not the star of the show. But when Iranians get a hold of it, we shove it on stage and make it sing. Silky pieces bob in a seaweed-green beef stew made with turmeric, onion, a little dried mint, and a big ol' handful of parsley. It's rich, tart, and so, so good—even better than your baba joon's (shhhhh).

ONION AND CELERY

- 4 tablespoons neutral oil, such as grapeseed or canola
- 1 medium yellow onion, cut into ½-inch dice
- 3 cups chopped (1-inch pieces) celery (about 9 stalks)
- ½ teaspoon Morton kosher salt
- 2 cups finely chopped flat-leaf parsley (from 2 bunches)
- 2 tablespoons dried mint

ASSEMBLY

- 2 tablespoons neutral oil, such as grapeseed or canola
- 1 medium yellow onion, cut into ½-inch dice
- 1 tablespoon ground turmeric
- 1 tablespoon freshly ground black pepper
- 2½ teaspoons Morton kosher salt, plus more to taste
- 1 pound beef chuck, cut into 1½-inch cubes
- Hot water, as needed
- ¼ cup fresh lemon juice (1 to 2 lemons)

FOR SERVING

- Maman's Saffron Rice (page 117)
- Mixed herbs (cilantro, mint leaves, and/or Persian or Thai basil)

Serves 4 to 6

COOK THE ONION AND CELERY: Heat 2 tablespoons of the oil in a large skillet over medium-high until it shimmers. Add the onion and cook, stirring occasionally, until browned at the edges, 4 to 6 minutes. Transfer to a bowl and set aside.

Set the skillet back on the heat, add the celery, salt, and remaining 2 tablespoons oil and stir well. Lower the heat to medium and cook, stirring occasionally, until the celery softens slightly, about 6 minutes.

Add the parsley, adjust the heat to low, and cook, stirring, until the celery is tender with a slight bite, about 8 minutes more. Remove from the heat, add the dried mint, and stir for a minute or so (to keep the mint from burning). Set aside.

ASSEMBLE THE DISH: Heat the oil in a 5- to 6-quart pot over medium-high until it shimmers. Add the onion and cook, stirring, until browned at the edges, 4 to 6 minutes. Stir in the turmeric, pepper, and 1 teaspoon of the salt.

Add the meat and ½ teaspoon of the salt and stir to coat. Cook, stirring, until the meat is lightly browned, about 5 minutes.

Add enough hot water to just submerge the meat (about 4 cups) and bring to a boil over high heat. Cover the pot (leave a tiny opening for steam to escape) and lower the heat to cook at a steady simmer, stirring occasionally, until the meat is tender, about 45 minutes.

Stir in the celery mixture and the remaining 1 teaspoon salt. Return to a simmer, then lower the heat to keep it at a simmer, again covered with a lil' opening, until the celery is fully tender and juicy, about 15 minutes.

Stir in the reserved onions and cook, uncovered, for 15 minutes, to meld the flavors and let it thicken up a bit. Season to taste with salt. Remove from the heat and squeeze on the lemon juice (Maman doesn't stir here and neither should you). Let it hang out for 5 minutes or so before eating. (Keeps in the fridge for up to 3 days. Reheat gently and add more lemon to taste.)

TO SERVE: Serve with saffron rice and herbs.

KHORESHT BADEMJOON

Eggplant 'n' Tomato Beef Stew

We Iranians genuinely use the eggplant emoji for innocent reasons—we're eggplant fiends. In this hearty dish, we caramelize them, peeled but whole, then plunk them along with tomatoes into an oniony, turmeric-tinged beef stew tarted up with musky, tangy black lime. Sliced tomatoes are classic, but sometimes we get freaky and add cherry tomatoes still on the vine.

- 7 tablespoons neutral oil, such as grapeseed or canola
- 2 medium yellow onions, cut into ½-inch dice
- 12 ounces beef chuck, cut into ½-inch cubes
- 4½ teaspoons Morton kosher salt
- 2 teaspoons ground turmeric
- 1 teaspoon freshly ground black pepper
- 6 tablespoons tomato paste
- 4 garlic cloves, finely chopped
- 1 whole dried black lime, poked a few times with a knife, or 1 teaspoon ground black lime
- 2¼ pounds Chinese or Japanese eggplants (about 8 small)
- 8 ounces tomatoes, cored and cut into ½-inch-thick rounds

FOR SERVING

- Maman's Saffron Rice (page 117)
- Mixed herbs (cilantro, mint leaves, and/or Persian or Thai basil)

Serves 4 to 6

Heat 4 tablespoons of the oil in a 6- to 8-quart Dutch oven over medium-high until it shimmers. Add the onions and cook, stirring occasionally, until browned at the edges, 7 to 8 minutes. Scoop out half the mixture and set aside for later.

Add 1 tablespoon of the oil, the meat, and ½ teaspoon of the salt to the pot and stir to coat well. Cook, stirring, until the meat is lightly browned, 2 to 3 minutes. Stir in the turmeric and pepper and cook, stirring, for 1 minute. Adjust the heat to medium-low and cook, scraping the pot, until it all turns a few shades darker and looks glossy, about 10 minutes more.

Make a little space for the tomato paste, add it along with the garlic, and cook, stirring frequently, until the paste turns a shade darker, about 5 minutes. Now stir everything together. Add the black lime and enough water to cover by about 1 inch (about 6 cups), increase the heat, and bring to a boil. Cover the pot (leave a tiny opening for steam to escape), lower the heat, and cook at a steady simmer, stirring occasionally, until the liquid has reduced to a saucy stew and the meat is very tender but not falling apart, about 1 hour 10 minutes.

Meanwhile, trim off the eggplants' leafy stems (but leave the nub). Peel the eggplants, then in the middle of each eggplant, make a 3-inch lengthwise slit through to the other side. Maman says this helps them cook evenly and not sog out. Put the eggplants on a large plate or tray, sprinkle all over with 1½ teaspoons of the salt, and let them hang out for 25 minutes to remove bitterness. Pat dry with paper towels.

Heat a large nonstick skillet over medium-high for a minute or so. Add the eggplants to the dry skillet and cook, undisturbed, until browned on the bottoms, about 4 minutes. Flip the eggplants, drizzle on the remaining 2 tablespoons oil, and cook, turning occasionally, until soft and deep golden brown all over, about 6 minutes. Transfer to a plate and set aside.

When the beef is ready, stir in the remaining 2½ teaspoons salt and lower the heat to cook at a gentle bubble. Lay the eggplants on the stew in a single layer, add the reserved onions evenly on top, then add the tomatoes in a single layer. Cook, uncovered and undisturbed, until the tomatoes are cooked through, about 10 minutes.

TO SERVE: Remove from the heat and let it hang out for 5 minutes or so before eating with rice and herbs.

KHORESHT GHEYMEH

Split Pea 'n' Beef Stew with Crispy Taters

Whether or not you've been lucky enough to try khoresht gheymeh before, it's going to taste cozy and comforting—it is, after all, a split pea stew with little hunks of tender beef. If you're green, though, you'll be especially tickled by the new-to-you symphony of deliciousness that comes when rose water and saffron meet cardamom and black limes. Crispy taters on top are the move.

- 3 tablespoons neutral oil, such as grapeseed or canola
- 1 large yellow onion, cut into ½-inch dice
- 1 teaspoon ground turmeric
- 1 teaspoon freshly ground black pepper
- 1 pound beef chuck, cut into 1½-inch cubes
- 2½ teaspoons Morton kosher salt
- 2 tablespoons tomato paste
- 6½ cups water
- 5 whole dried black limes, poked a few times with a knife, or 5 teaspoons ground black lime
- 1 cup yellow split peas
- 3 tablespoons Saffron Water (it's easy—see page 19)
- 1 tablespoon fresh lemon juice
- 1 tablespoon rose water
- 1 teaspoon ground cardamom, preferably black
- 1 teaspoon ground cinnamon

FOR SERVING

- Crispy Taters (recipe follows)
- Maman's Saffron Rice (page 117)
- Mixed herbs (cilantro, mint leaves, and/or Persian or Thai basil)

Serves 4 to 6

Heat the oil in a medium pot over medium-high until it shimmers. Add the onion and cook, stirring occasionally, until browned at the edges, 4 to 6 minutes. Transfer about one-quarter of the onions to a bowl and set aside.

Stir in the turmeric and pepper. Add the meat and 1½ teaspoons of the salt and stir to coat. Cook, stirring, until the meat is lightly browned, about 5 minutes. Add the tomato paste and stir for 1 minute or so. Adjust the heat to medium, add ½ cup of the water and cook, stirring and scraping the pot, for 1 minute more.

Add the black limes and remaining 6 cups water, then bring to a boil over high heat. Cover the pot (leave a tiny opening for steam to escape) and adjust the heat to cook at a gentle simmer, stirring occasionally, until the meat is tender, about 1½ hours.

When the meat is tender, stir in the split peas, saffron water, lemon juice, rose water, cardamom, cinnamon, and remaining 1 teaspoon salt. Stir and simmer, still covered, until the split peas are tender but not mushy and the liquid has thickened slightly, about 30 minutes.

TO SERVE: Top with the reserved sautéed onions and crispy taters. Serve rice and herbs on the side.

CRISPY TATERS

Make these while the stew stews.

- Neutral oil, such as grapeseed or canola
- 1 pound Yukon Gold potatoes, peeled and cut into ¼-inch-thick French fries
- Kosher salt
- 1½ teaspoons Saffron Water (it's easy—see page 19)

Serves 4 to 6

Line a large bowl with paper towels. Pour 2 inches of neutral oil into a medium Dutch oven and heat over high until the oil bubbles furiously when you dip a piece of potato (or until it reaches 350°F).

Working in two batches, fry the potatoes, stirring occasionally, until fully crisp and golden brown, 6 to 8 minutes.

Transfer to the bowl, sprinkle with salt, and drizzle with the saffron water. Tossy tossy.

ABGOOSHT

Meat 'n' Potato Mash with Broth—aka Persian Birria

Abgoosht—ab is water, goosht is meat—is bone broth before the influencers ruined it. Actually, it's even cooler than that. You stew the goosht with potatoes and warm spices, then you siphon off the broth, and mash the meat and spuds. Maman often makes it with lamb, but insists it's even better with sheep (aka mutton).

Serve it all with herbs, torshi, and raw onions. Use bread or tortillas to make little taquitos and either dunk them in the broth (or slurp some between bites). The same way you'd eat Mexican birria.

- 5 tablespoons neutral oil, such as grapeseed or canola
- 1¼ pounds lamb loin chops (5 or 6)
- 1 medium white onion, cut into ¼-inch cubes
- 3 teaspoons Morton kosher salt
- ½ teaspoon ground turmeric
- ½ teaspoon freshly ground black pepper
- 2 tablespoons tomato paste
- 8 ounces tomatoes (about 2), cut into ½-inch dice
- 4 cups water
- 1 cup drained canned beans (preferably a mix of white beans and chickpeas)
- 3 medium Yukon Gold potatoes, peeled and quartered
- 3 dried black limes, poked a few times with a knife, or 1 tablespoon ground black lime
- 1 cinnamon stick
- Pinch of red pepper flakes

FOR SERVING

- Mixed herbs (cilantro, mint leaves, and/or Persian or Thai basil)
- Torshi (page 174)
- Thinly sliced onions
- Noon Barbari (page 125), store-bought lavash, or Duck-Fat Flour Tortillas (page 189)

Serves 4 or 5

Heat the oil in a large Dutch oven or other wide pot over medium-high until it shimmers. Add the lamb chops, onion, 1 teaspoon of the salt, the turmeric, and pepper and cook, stirring and flipping the chops, until the meat and onion are a little golden, about 10 minutes.

Add the tomato paste and cook, stirring, for 1 minute. Add the tomatoes and cook for 2 minutes more. Add the water, remaining 2 teaspoons salt, the beans, potatoes, limes, cinnamon, and pepper flakes and bring to a boil. Partially cover, lower the heat, and cook at a moderate simmer until the potatoes and lamb are very tender, about 1½ hours.

Set a large mesh sieve over a big bowl and carefully pour in the abgoosht. Reserve the broth in the bowl and return the solids to the pot. Pick the meat from the bones, discarding the bones and the cinnamon stick. If you used whole black limes, transfer them to a little side bowl, for the nibblers. Using a blunt object, like the wooden mallet thingie that exists only in Persian households or more likely a potato masher, turn the solids (meat, spuds, beans, and all) to a coarse mash.

TO SERVE: Go family style, and set out the pot of mash, the bowl of broth, and plates or bowls with herbs, torshi, onions, and your pick of something round, flat, and chewy. Have everyone dig in.

GHORMEH SABZI

Kidney Bean 'n' Beef Herby McHerbison Stew

The queen of Persian stews, she's a crowd favorite—chunks of tender beef and purple-y kidney beans and fragrant black limes, all wading in a sea of herbs. No, seriously, look at the ingredients. Those numbers are not typos. Maman adds handfuls . . . no, heaps . . . no, mountains of parsley, cilantro, and scallions to the pot, and they transform into the rich, olive green body of this stew. Spend two seconds in a kitchen where it's simmering away and the aroma will permeate your clothes, skin, and soul.

- 5 tablespoons neutral oil, such as grapeseed or canola
- 1 large yellow onion, thinly sliced
- 1 tablespoon ground turmeric
- 3 teaspoons Morton kosher salt, plus more to taste
- 1 teaspoon freshly ground black pepper
- 1½ pounds beef chuck, cut into 1½-inch cubes
- 5 bunches of scallions
- 5 bunches of flat-leaf parsley
- 2 bunches of cilantro
- 4 dried black limes, poked a few times with a knife, or 4 teaspoons ground black lime
- One 15-ounce can kidney beans, drained and rinsed
- 2 tablespoons dried fenugreek leaves (shambalileh)
- 1 teaspoon Saffron Water (it's easy—see page 19)

FOR SERVING

- Maman's Saffron Rice (page 117)
- Mixed herbs (cilantro, mint leaves, and/or Persian or Thai basil)

Serves 4 to 6

Heat 2 tablespoons of the oil in a 5- to 6-quart pot over medium-high until it shimmers. Add the onion and cook, stirring, until browned at the edges, 4 to 6 minutes.

Add the turmeric, 1 teaspoon of the salt, and the pepper and cook for 1 minute. Add the beef and another teaspoon of the salt, stir well, and cook, stirring, until the meat is lightly browned, 8 to 10 minutes.

Add enough water (about 4 cups) to just submerge the meat by 1 inch and bring to a boil over high heat. Partially cover the pot and lower the heat to cook at a gentle simmer, stirring occasionally, until the meat is tender, about 1½ hours.

Meanwhile, trim and thinly slice the scallions and pop them in a big bowl. Trim all but 1 inch of the stems from the parsley and cilantro, then either by hand or in a food processor, chop them finely and add them to the bowl.

Heat the remaining 3 tablespoons oil in a large skillet over medium until it shimmers. Add the herb mixture and cook, stirring frequently, for 20 minutes, to give the herbs time to meld.

When the beef is ready, add the herb mixture, black limes, beans, the remaining 1 teaspoon salt, and ½ cup water. Bring to a boil, then cover the pot and lower the heat to cook at a gentle simmer until dark green and thickened, about 50 minutes. Stir in the fenugreek leaves, cover, and cook for 10 minutes more.

Stir in the saffron water. If the stew is still soupy, continue to cook, uncovered, until it's nice and thick. If you used whole black limes, transfer them to a little side bowl, for the nibblers. Season to taste with salt.

TO SERVE: Serve with saffron rice and, yeah, seriously, the fresh herbs.

FESENJOON

Pomegranate 'n' Walnut Stew—aka Persian Mole

Sexy to look at? No. Will you be devouring every last bite of the ugly-delicious masterpiece? Damn straight. Complexly flavored with fruit, nuts, and spices, it's our version of those Mexican moles—rich and tangy, silky and just laborious enough to bust out when your in-laws come through, though notably not as laborious to make as the sauces favored by Edgar's peeps.

Maman makes hers with the little cutie-pie meatballs (aka ghelghely) you see here, but we've been known to swap them out for the duck carnitas (see page 225), a nod to the fesenjoons of old that were made with duck but also because it's SO GOOD. If you do, add the shredded duck 5 to 10 minutes or so after you add the saffron water.

- 2 medium yellow onions, peeled but whole
- 1 pound ground beef, preferably 80/20
- 6 teaspoons Morton kosher salt
- ½ teaspoon freshly ground black pepper
- ½ teaspoon ground turmeric
- ¼ cup neutral oil, such as grapeseed or canola
- 1 pound raw walnuts
- 3 cups water
- 1 cup pomegranate molasses
- 5 tablespoons sugar
- 1 tablespoon tomato paste
- 1 tablespoon Saffron Water (it's easy—see page 19)

FOR SERVING

- Pomegranate seeds
- Maman's Saffron Rice (page 117)
- Mixed herbs (cilantro, mint leaves, and/or Persian or Thai basil)

Serves 4 or 5

Grate the onions on a box grater directly onto a kitchen towel. Gather the edges, hold it over the sink, and squeeze out as much liquid as you can.

In a medium bowl, combine the beef, 1 teaspoon of the salt, the pepper, turmeric, and half of the onions. Mix to distribute the ingredients well, about 2 minutes. Use damp hands to form 1-inch meatballs and transfer to a tray or plate.

Heat the oil in a large pot over medium until it shimmers. Working in batches to avoid overcrowding, cook the meatballs, turning occasionally, until browned all over, 3 to 4 minutes per batch. Transfer them to a tray or plate as they're fried, leaving the fat behind.

Meanwhile, buzz those walnuts in a food processor until finely ground (on the verge of nut butter!).

When all the meatballs are fried and on the tray, decrease the heat to low, then add the remaining onions and the ground walnuts. Cook, stirring occasionally, until it gets darker and a little thicker, 4 to 5 minutes. Add the water and stir gently for a few minutes.

Stir in the pomegranate molasses, sugar, and tomato paste. Increase the heat and bring to a simmer. Cover, lower the heat, and simmer gently, stirring occasionally to prevent the bottom from burning, until gravy thick and glossy, 40 to 45 minutes.

Stir in the meatballs, saffron water, and the remaining 5 teaspoons salt. Return to a simmer, then cover and cook at a gentle simmer again, to cook the meatballs through and meld the flavors, about 20 minutes.

TO SERVE: Let it hang out, uncovered, for 10 minutes or so. Serve sprinkled with the pomegranate seeds alongside saffron rice.

MAHICHE

Braised Lamb Shanks

Onions, turmeric, and a few hours of hands-off simmering turn lamb shanks into a showstopper wading in a broth that doubles as a miracle drug. It heals all, I swear. Mahiche is a decadent, meaty pleasure that you can eat with bread. But Maman's going to maman, so she serves it with a heap of baghali polo, which is rice packed with dill and fava beans.

- 3 pounds lamb shanks (2 large or 4 small)
- 2 medium red onions, 1 quartered, 1 thinly sliced
- 8 tablespoons neutral oil, such as grapeseed or canola
- 2 tablespoons ground turmeric
- 1 tablespoon freshly ground black pepper
- 2 teaspoons Morton kosher salt, plus more to taste
- 4 garlic cloves, roughly chopped
- 2 bay leaves

FOR SERVING

- Baghali Polo (page 118)
- Mixed herbs (cilantro, mint leaves, and/or Persian or Thai basil)

Serves 4

In a medium pot, combine the shanks, the quartered onion, 5 tablespoons of the oil, 1 tablespoon of the turmeric, the pepper, 1 teaspoon of the salt, the garlic, bay leaves, and enough water to cover by 1 inch. Bring to a boil, then partially cover and lower the heat to cook at a gentle simmer until the lamb is very tender but not falling apart, 2 to 3 hours.

Transfer the shanks to a plate. If the liquid hasn't reduced by about half, simmer it some more. Strain the cooking liquid into a separate container, discarding the solids, and stir in the remaining 1 teaspoon salt.

Heat 2 tablespoons of the oil in a large skillet (preferably nonstick) over medium-high until it shimmers. Add the sliced onion and cook, stirring occasionally, until browned at the edges, 4 to 6 minutes. Stir in the remaining 1 tablespoon turmeric.

Push the onions to the side. Add the remaining 1 tablespoon oil, then the lamb shanks, and cook, flipping once, until golden brown on both sides, about 6 minutes total.

Pour in 1½ cups of the reserved cooking liquid and cook, basting the shanks with the liquid and onions, for 10 minutes. Cover and cook for 10 minutes more, until the lamb is falling off the bone. Season with salt to taste.

TO SERVE: Serve on a platter with the remaining cooking liquid in bowls, the baghali polo, and herbs on the side.

BAGHLAVA

Y'all Know the Drill

Maman can be tight-lipped about her cooking. The first time Edgar ate her unmatched baghlava, he asked, in awe, why on earth it was so good. She laughed. She demurred. Then at last, she whispered, "Saffron." It's true that her generous hand with the good stuff gives her baghlava an especially savory character. And yet she happily uses any old frozen phyllo dough. She's high-low like that.

NUT MIXTURE

2 cups raw walnuts
2 cups raw almonds
2 cups raw pecans
½ cup sugar
1 teaspoon ground cardamom, preferably black

ASSEMBLY

1½ cups water
1½ cups sugar
2 tablespoons Saffron Water (it's easy—see page 19)
½ cup rose water
10 ounces (2½ sticks) unsalted butter, melted
One 1-pound package phyllo dough (18 by 13-inch sheets), thawed if frozen

Serves 10

MAKE THE NUT MIXTURE: Working in batches if necessary, grind the nuts in a food processor to the texture of bread crumbs—aka nice and fluffy but with a little texture. Transfer to a medium bowl, add the sugar and cardamom, and mix well. Set aside.

ASSEMBLE THE BAGHLAVA: In a small saucepan, bring the water to a simmer over high heat. Add the sugar and bring to a boil, stirring to dissolve the sugar. Immediately decrease the heat to low, then stir in the saffron water, and then the rose water. Keep warm until ready to use.

Brush the bottom and sides of an 18 by 13-inch sheet pan with butter. Add 1 sheet of phyllo to the pan, letting the edges go slightly up the sides of the pan if necessary. Generously brush the sides, edges, and corners of the sheet with melted butter, then brush on a smattering over the rest of the sheet. Repeat with 3 more sheets of phyllo.

Add an even layer of the nut mixture (about 2 cups), then repeat the layers—4 buttered phyllo sheets, nuts, 4 buttered phyllo sheets, nuts.

Now you're going to add the final 4 sheets of phyllo but you're going to butter them a lil' differently. Add a sheet of phyllo to the nuts and brush lightly with butter. Flip the sheet onto the nuts and brush with butter as you did with the other phyllo sheets, paying special attention to the sides, edges, and corners. Repeat with 3 more sheets. If you have any butter left over, brush it over the top.

Use a table knife to cut the baghlava lengthwise into strips 2 inches wide (or 1 inch wide, if you want more pieces), holding the phyllo in place with your free hand. Next, diagonally cut the baghlava to make diamonds (okay, more like parallelograms).

COOK THE BAGHLAVA: Preheat the oven to 375°F. Put a rack in the lowest position and one in the top position.

Drizzle about ⅔ cup of the saffron syrup over the baghlava, paying special attention to getting it in the cuts and edges.

CONTINUED

Bake for 20 minutes, drizzling with saffron syrup every 5 minutes until it's all gone.

Keep baking until it's puffy, crispy, and golden brown on top, 35 to 40 minutes, rotating the pan once or twice. Transfer the baklava to the top rack and turn on the broiler. Broil, checking and rotating the pan frequently, until the top is deep golden brown, 1 to 2 minutes.

Let it cool to room temp, about 2 hours, slapping away fiends who will try and eat it before it's cooled.

TO SERVE: Remove the pieces one at a time, recutting the slits and using a fork or offset spatula to very carefully remove pieces from the pan. (Keeps in an airtight container on the counter for up to 1 week.)

YOGURT, PICKLES, DRINKS, AND STUFF

AGHA REZA'S MAST

Yogurt

An average Tuesday eve for an Iranian girl: sitting around the kitchen table with your maman, baba, cousins, aunt, and Agha Reza and talking (read: yelling) about yogurt. They all think their way is best, that their particular minor deviation from the basic process leads to yogurt that's superior because it's thinner, thicker, more sour, more viscous. None of them are wrong. That said, my uncle Agha Reza's yogurt reigns supreme—the silkiest of all, with just the right tang. This recipe reflects his technique, and the result refutes the family's protestation that it's not his method but his legendary mustache that makes his yogurt so good.

As Agha Reza likes to remind me, "Without mast, you can't make mast." Philosophical! Also true. This recipe for yogurt does require yogurt, so buy a good one—it shouldn't just claim to contain active cultures but should taste like it does, you know? For subsequent batches, use the yogurt you made yourself.

½ gallon whole milk
⅓ cup plain yogurt, whisked well

Makes about 6½ cups

In a medium pot, bring the milk to a gentle simmer over medium-low heat, about 30 minutes, then simmer gently for 1 hour. No stirring needed.

Turn off the heat and let it cool until it registers 100°F on a thermometer (my family doesn't mess around), about 1 hour. (You could also dip a finger: 100°F feels lukewarm, just above body temperature.) Add the yogurt and whisk until smooth, then immediately cover with a tight-fitting lid.

Drape a nice thick kitchen towel over the lid and leave it at room temp until it thickens and develops a delectable tang, 36 to 48 hours, depending on your room's temperature.

Transfer the mast into containers—glass is fab; Maman uses a mini amphora clay pot—and refrigerate, uncovered and overnight, so it thickens up a little more. (Keeps in the fridge for up to 10 days.)

NANA DAGH

Fried Mint Oil

Woweee, more herbs! This time, though, instead of fresh by the bushel, it's dried, concentrated mint infused into oil for punchy, aromatic drizzle on Aush Reshteh (page 139) or other thangs.

½ cup neutral oil, such as grapeseed or canola
2 tablespoons dried mint

Makes about ½ cup

Heat the oil in a small saucepan over medium-high until it shimmers.

Add the mint, stir, then remove from the heat. Let the mint steep for 10 minutes.

You can use it right away, but for best flavor, let it cool completely, then pour into a container (mint and all) and refrigerate overnight. (Keeps in the fridge for up to 1 month.)

ZERESHK

Tangy-Sweet Barberries

Here's how Maman turns unassuming dried barberries—itty-bitty fruits the size of currants that taste like the sour-sweet love child of a cranberry and a raisin—into an electric topping for Tachin (page 127) or the saffron rice in Zereshk Polo ba Morgh (page 144). For maximum drip, look for ruby-colored barberries, though the dark ones taste great, too. The buttery liquid makes a great rice drizzle.

1 small yellow onion
3½ tablespoons unsalted butter, cut into a few pieces
1 tablespoon neutral oil, such as grapeseed or canola
1 cup (about 3 ounces) zereshk (dried barberries), rinsed well
3 tablespoons sugar
2 tablespoons Saffron Water (it's easy—see page 19)
1 tablespoon rose water

Makes about 1½ cups

Grate the onion on the large holes of a box grater. Melt the butter in a medium skillet over medium heat. Add the oil and onion and cook, stirring frequently, until the onions begin to brown, about 5 minutes. Stir in the zereshk and cook just until warmed through, about 1 minute.

Add the sugar and stir constantly for 30 seconds. Add the saffron water and rose water and stir for 30 seconds more. Turn off the heat and stir for another 30 seconds. Cover to keep warm. (Keeps in the fridge for up to 3 days. Gently warm before serving.)

ZEYTOON PARVARDEH

Savory Pomegranate 'n' Walnut Olives

On our epic trip to Iran, Edgar and I fell for this stunner of a party snack in Gilan, the northern province where my mamani comes from. It's olives marinated with crushed walnuts, pomegranate molasses, and herbs. We use pecans in place of walnuts since they're native to Texas, and we use mint instead of the classic chuchagh, because come on, where the hell are you getting chuchagh?

Generous 1 cup raw pecans or walnuts
2 cups (12 ounces) unpitted Castelvetrano olives, rinsed
1 cup mint leaves, chopped
2 tablespoons minced garlic (about 6 cloves)
½ cup plus 2 tablespoons pomegranate molasses
4 tablespoons extra-virgin olive oil
1 teaspoon Morton kosher salt

Serves 6 to 8

In a food processor, buzz the pecans until they're like coarse sand, about 15 seconds.

In a medium bowl, combine the pecans, olives, mint, and garlic and mix well. Add the pomegranate, olive oil, and salt and mix well.

Cover and marinate in the fridge for at least 12 hours and up to 10 days (they get better with time). Before serving, bring the mixture to room temperature.

SHOORI

Salty Pickles—aka Persian Escabeche

Perfect for snacking and sandwiches, this low-effort pickle is a mix of crunchy veg. Classically, it's carrots, cauliflower, celery, jalapeño, and so much garlic, though all are welcome in the salt and vinegar brine tinged with anise-y dried tarragon. If you don't want to make them, buy them!

3½ cups sliced (½ inch thick) peeled carrots (about 8)
2 cups sliced (½ inch thick) celery
7 jalapeño chiles, sliced ½ inch thick
7 cups small cauliflower florets (1 medium head)
1 cup peeled garlic cloves (about 40)
¾ cup (0.6 ounce/18g) dried tarragon
8 cups lukewarm water
2 cups distilled white vinegar
6 tablespoons Morton kosher salt

Makes about 5 quarts

In a large bowl, combine the carrots, celery, jalapeños, cauliflower, garlic, and tarragon and toss well. Divide the mixture among narrow containers like jars.

In a large container, combine the lukewarm water, vinegar, and salt and stir to dissolve the salt. Pour just enough of the mixture into the jars to submerge the vegetables. A few might bob at the surface, but they'll sink once they start absorbing the brine.

Let pickle in the fridge for at least 1 week or up to 1 month.

TORSHI

Sour Relish—aka Persian Giardiniera

My family does torshi a little differently. In other homes and in grocery stores, this punchy pickle comes in big hunks. The Mardanbigis, on the other hand, chop the array of veg finely, like Chicago-style giardiniera, which makes it easy to use judiciously. That's important, because it's an umami-vinegar bomb.

I know what you're wondering: Can you leave out the golpar and the marze? (Great pronunciation, by the way!) Sure, but you're going to miss golpar's bitter, earthy vibes and marze's peppery, woodsy quality. The black sesame? That's my family's touch, so omit at your own risk.

1 medium head cauliflower (about 2 pounds)
2 medium-large carrots (about 10 ounces), peeled
2 medium globe eggplants (about 1¾ pounds total)
3 Persian (mini) cucumbers (about 10 ounces)
6 celery stalks (about 10 ounces total)
1 medium shallot, peeled
1 jalapeño chile
1 Granny Smith apple (about 8 ounces), peeled and cored
8 garlic cloves, peeled
3 tablespoons Morton kosher salt
1 tablespoon marze (dried savory)
1 tablespoon dried mint
1 tablespoon dried dill
1 tablespoon dried tarragon
4 teaspoons ground golpar (Persian hogweed seeds or, erroneously, "angelica seeds")
1 tablespoon ground turmeric
1 tablespoon freshly ground black pepper
1 tablespoon ground cumin
2 teaspoons black sesame seeds
2 teaspoons ground celery seed
5 cups apple cider vinegar

Makes 10 cups

Chop all the vegetables, apple, and garlic into tiny pieces (shoot for ⅛ inch). Knife only, sorry—the food processor would make mush. Transfer the chopped stuff to a big bowl.

Add the salt, dried herbs, ground spices, sesame seeds, and ground celery seed and toss to mix really well. Add the vinegar and stir well. Press down so everything's submerged in the liquid. If necessary, put a piece of plastic wrap on the surface and add a weight to keep it all submerged or transfer to a narrower container.

Cover tightly and set aside at room temp, stirring once or twice, for 24 hours.

Spoon the vegetables into mason jars, then pour the brine evenly into each jar. Cover tightly and refrigerate for at least 1 week before eating. (Keeps in the fridge—and gets better and better—for up to 6 months, though I've enjoyed torshi that's as old as a toddler.)

SHARBAT

Tart-Sweet Bevvie

Whether you're facing down the heat of Austin or Ahvaz, the key to cooling down happily is sharbat, like a Persian agua fresca. It's jazzed-up sweet syrup mixed with something tart and some bubbly water, then served over ice. In fact, it's the OG refresher, the forebear of sherbet and way easier to make.

Sharbat knows no bounds. For the tart component, you can use whatever you've got, from verjus to lemon juice to mashed-up blackberries. For the flavorings, try subtly floral rose petals and saffron, or an herby sitch, like the licorice-y, pleasantly astringent yarrow that grows all over Texas. Or go wild with whatever's handy.

The recipe makes enough syrup for 16 drinks, but you can make as few as one at a time.

SYRUP

1 cup sugar
1 cup water
¼ cup distilled white vinegar

FLAVORING 1

2 tablespoons dried rose petals
½ teaspoon Saffron Water (it's easy—see page 19)

FLAVORING 2

Small handful of mint, tarragon leaves, or yarrow

PER DRINK

Plenty of ice
¼ cup white verjus, lemon juice, white wine vinegar, or orange juice
1½ tablespoons syrup (from above)
½ cup sparkling water, preferably Topo Chico

Makes 16 drinks

MAKE THE SYRUP: In a small pot, combine the sugar, water, vinegar, and flavoring 1 or 2. Set over medium heat and cook, stirring, just until the sugar dissolves, about 4 minutes.

Let cool, strain, and store the syrup in the fridge for up to 1 week.

MAKE THE DRINK: In ice-filled glasses, combine the verjus and syrup, top with the sparkling water, and stir well before serving.

DOOGH

Savory 'n' Tangy Yogurt Bevvie

Iranians are trailblazers. To the massive list of stuff Persians pioneered, you can add beverage pairings. This savory, fizzy yogurt drink is pretty much the perfect match for rich and/or charred dishes, like Baba's Kabob (page 147).

4 cups Agha Reza's Mast (page 169) or any good tangy yogurt
2 cups still or sparkling water (your preference), cold
1½ teaspoons dried mint, or more to taste
1 teaspoon Morton kosher salt
Ice cubes
1 tablespoon dried rose petals (optional)

Serves 4 to 6

Put the mast in a serving pitcher and leave it out, covered, at room temp for 24 hours. It'll get even more sour. That's good.

Chill the mast in the pitcher for up to 2 days.

Just before serving, stir in the water, dried mint, and salt and mix well. Serve cold over ice and garnished with the rose petals.

"So . . . what are you?"

Translation: You don't look like you're from here, and I'm perplexed.

—SO MANY PEOPLE, TO BOTH OF US

AMERICA

RECIPES FROM A LIL' TAQUERIA
IN AUSTIN, TEJAS

Topo Chico
Topo Chico

SARA: Oh, America. You big, dumb, beautiful goof. You're the only place Nixta could be. The only country where Edgar and I, first-gen immigrants whose families are from so far away, could find each other, fall in love, and create something bigger than just us. It's the place where people hate us and where people love us, where people take care of us and where we take care of them. You've never been more insane, but we love you still.

EDGAR: Sara and I are both seekers. I found cooking after an injury derailed my dreams of playing football and I took a job making Caesars and grilling rib eyes at Tahoe Joe's, a steakhouse in Visalia. I loved cooking and tried on many toques before I found my way. Sara is like a leaf in the wind, blown around by life but quietly guided by her heart, intuition, and the encouragement of her family. They told her her mind must be cherished, and she could do or be anything. Her first real job, at fourteen years old, was crew trainer at a McDonald's in Arkansas. Now, she's the sort-of big-boss crew trainer at Nixta.

SARA: My baba is also a seeker. While Maman was the upholder of tradition, my steady link to my past, Baba was restless. He came here to go to school, dabbled as an importer/exporter of Iranian goods, then opened an improbable cafe in rural Arkansas called Friendly's. It sold gas, convenience store bits and bobs, and a 15-minute oil change. It also sold biscuits and gravy, chicken-fried steak, and fried okra. You know, traditional Persian fare.

He closed up shop as his construction business took off. Baba helped build a whole new neighborhood in Northwest Arkansas, a metropolitan area that goes by the acronym—hilarious to Edgar, a major hip-hop fan—of NWA. In the neighborhood Baba built, there's a street named Bigi and another named Ghamar, my mom's name. God knows how the locals pronounce them, but he literally made his mark.

Edgar's dad, Fermin, might have been the breadwinner, eventually buying their home and saving enough to care for his parents. But Edgar's mom, Flor, found her way, too. She worked those long shifts as a cleaner to pay for school. She worked a full-time job, raised a family, and through all that sought something more, becoming a dental hygienist in her thirties.

EDGAR: I was still seeking when I met Sara. I'd already had my light-switch moment with corn, but I very much didn't have the space, money, or operational know-how to make my taqueria happen. I did know one thing: Austin was the place. Ten years before, I had visited the city and left with the impression it was just a small town. Now I could tell. Austin was on the cusp. It was about to blow up.

Not only that, the capital of Tejas was well-versed in Mexican food and already familiar with cultural mash-ups—the queso, breakfast tacos, brisket tacos, migas, all of it born from the minds of Tejanos, Mexican-Americans who learned to cook with what was available in Texas. It was wild to go from one very Mexican place, like LA, to another Mexican(ish) place, like Austin, and for the Mexican food in each place to be so different. It was similar to the experience of traveling within Mexico itself—the cochinita pibil, the lobster burritos, the rainbow of moles, from yellow to red to midnight black, all so different and all so Mexican. The good news for me: My nixtamal-centered project would be a relative novelty in a city where the dominant tortilla was flour. In LA, corn was king. In Austin, there was plenty of room for me and my food.

When I took that fateful catering gig, it was a way to make ends meet, but also a way to scope out the city, to get to know the landscape of local folks you need to procure everything from prime Angus beef to Cambros to napkins. Then she walked in. Sara just had this aura to her. I was like, Damn, this girl is cool. That night, I might have done a little Insta stalking and upgraded her in my mind to, Damn, this girl is really cool.

SARA: Edgar's first week there was my last. We made some googly-eyes at each other, I went on a month's sabbatical, then I slid into those DMs. And that was that. As one does with their new boo, Edgar told me all about his dream of a restaurant. And for a couple years, it stayed a dream because, and I'm not sure if you've heard, opening a restaurant is a real motherfucker. I was all for it and down to support him in any way I could, as long as it didn't interfere with my day job. At the time, I was working as Senior Talent Engagement Manager (totally normal job title) for a local taco minichain. I made pretty good money. I had insurance! You know, living the dream.

EDGAR: While I was hustling to open, Sara served as a sort of unofficial advisor. Then an Eater article dropped. We were super stoked—the first real buzz for Nixta. The story was all, There's this LA chef who worked at Trois Mec and Son of a Gun and Pujol. Now he's opening a chilled-out taqueria on Dozen Street. It was a lucky break. It was exciting. It got Sara fired.

SARA: He's right. The article called me a partner and in the same breath mentioned my current employer. I got called into corporate. The article coincided with some corporate reshuffling and my new boss wasn't having it.

EDGAR: Sara was devastated. Not just because she was the only one in the couple with insurance and a steady paycheck, but also because Sara is the most on-it person I've ever met. Her emails, whether to vendors or strangers or local government officials, are as thoughtful and well-informed as they are poetic. She has an innate sense of feng shui, stepping into a room and knowing immediately if anything isn't in just the right place. Ask her to do something by Tuesday and it's done by . . . okay, it's done by Tuesday, because she's really freaking busy. In hindsight, her getting canned was probably the best thing that could have happened. Because now we were full-on in this project together.

SARA: I was sad. I was scared. But I was also more motivated than ever to prove something. I believed in Edgar's vision for the food a thousand percent. Broadly speaking, its spirit is something old mixed with something new, tortillas made the ancient way topped with food that reflected Edgar's life experience. He makes exactly what you might expect a Mexican-American with a French, Californian, and Japanese culinary background, not to mention an Iranian-American shorty, to cook. You know, American food. It's thoughtful, silly, and most important, so damn tasty. As Edgar tells it, anything can be a taco. And when you grow up eating virtually everything along with a pile of steamy tortillas, everything eventually does.

EDGAR: My food is cool and all, but Sara is the force that makes Nixta so dope. She also brings something old—that Persian hospitality, a deep-rooted desire to make people feel fed and taken care of, whether that's with heaps of fluffy saffron-tinted rice or piles of steamy tortillas. She merges that old-school welcome with her sassy charm. Maman has sky-high standards for rice. Sara has the same sky-high standards for fun—from the backyard bubble machines to secret Lil Wayne photos in the bathroom.

She also brought her food. Thanks to her, my arroz con leche (cinnamon-spiked Mexican rice pudding) merged with sholeh zard (saffron-spiked Iranian rice pudding) to become one of our biggest hits. The dessert had some of my abuela, who hawked the dish back home in California as a post-retirement hustle. It had some of Sara's maman, who made sholeh zard on special occasions to share with neighbors. And it had some of that first-gen flair—the dose of butter and egg yolks I picked up in French kitchens, and pulverized freeze-dried strawberries for a little pop of acidity and color.

Despite the distance between the countries where our families came from, there was more overlap than just rice pudding. The food of Mexico and the Middle East have many more moments of convergence. Al pastor in Mexico has roots in shawarma, both are marinated meats cooking on vertical spits. From Puebla to Mexico City, you'll find that meat served on tortillas—or on pitas, when it's called tacos arabes (Arab tacos). In the Yucatán, you'll find kibis, fried meat-and-bulgur dumplings found in Levantine cuisine (and called kibbeh), served in the local fashion with pickled red onion, shredded cabbage, and habaneros. It was no wonder when Sara tasted mole, she said

it reminded her of Iranian fesenjoon, both rich sauces made from nuts, fruit, and spices.

SARA: Edgar and I learned that these moments of overlap aren't random. When the Spanish colonized Mexico, in the sixteenth century, Spain had been ruled for eight centuries by the Moors, Arab and Berber Muslims from North Africa. In the late nineteenth to the mid-twentieth century, immigrants from Lebanon and Syria bolstered this strand of culinary commingling. The reasons were often brutal and ugly. The results, with the luxury of distance and time, are beautiful. The foods Edgar and I grew up on were decidedly different but impossible to untangle. We embraced it. We made fesenjoon, put it on Edgar's incredible tortillas, and called it a Persian mole taco.

EDGAR: We're getting ahead of ourselves, Sara. We haven't even opened yet. And that probably wouldn't have gone so well if it hadn't been for Mariam. Mariam Parker was the hardworking (Persian!) executive director of a nonprofit called Austin Food & Wine Alliance, which provides grants and scholarships to support local food entrepreneurs, and now someone we call a friend.

We'd only signed our lease a few months before Mariam invited us to cook at the Live Fire Festival. Next thing we know, there we were cooking beside some of the city's coolest chefs. A few booths down from us, for example, was Aaron Franklin, the man behind the legendarily delicious Franklin Barbecue. We fed the brisket maven a beef tartare tostada with a mole-cured egg, and he liked it enough to give us a spot at his Hot Luck Festival. Our luck cascaded, one break leading to another until food publications were heralding a scrappy, as-yet-unopened taqueria as the hottest opening in the country.

SARA: Luck was part of Edgar's and my journey, for sure. It connected the dots that formed our promising trajectory. But it was community that created those dots in the first place. It was the people who welcomed us, who for no good reason gave us their advice, time, and support, who became collaborators and friends.

From go, nurturing a sense of community was vital for us. We were opening in a Black and Brown neighborhood, and despite not exactly being pale ourselves, we knew what customers we'd likely attract with our carrot tostadas and duck tacos. We decided we had to preserve the spirit of the little cinder block building, which has been there since 1965 and has been everything from a convenience store to a barber shop. The large backyard, we decided, wouldn't just be for us. It would be for everyone: The site of a community garden, for pop-ups for friends trying to start businesses, for voting registration drives, for block parties, and for the birthday shindig for one of our favorite neighbors, who's lived in this neck of the woods for way longer than we have.

Because buzz doesn't pay bills, we were grinding every day (figuratively and literally with the corn and our aging joints) to get this place open, our bank account balance dwindling by the hour. Our community kept us going during the many difficult moments on the unpaved road to opening the restaurant and on the freaking Autobahn to staying open. The curious neighbors who came by to see who was taking over the little cafe on Dozen Street and who ended up grabbing paint brushes. The friends, old and new, who helped us execute the YouTube tutorials on wiring lights, tiling walls, and building a bar.

The day we passed the final building inspection and got the official bureaucratic okay to open, the bank account was down to three digits. If Nixta didn't hit from the jump, we'd be in trouble.

Suddenly we started to wonder if people were right that we were nuts for signing a lease on 12th and Cedar. At the time, there were only a couple of restaurants on Dozen Street, including a place called Sam's Barbecue. (Their slogan: You don't need no teeth to eat my beef.) Sam's opened in 1940 and it's still kicking. When we finally opened, there was a line snaking down the block at Nixta, and we never had to worry about anything ever again.

If only.

Nonrestaurant folks don't always realize this, but a packed restaurant is not the same as a successful one. Margins are slim. Buzz dies down. Roofs leak. City officials decide to make you repermit, strong-arming you to partially shut down for seven hellish months. But there we were, trying our best, really trying to love on our guests and keep them. Five months in, we were celebrating. After all, we had just had our best month yet. That was February 2020.

Through it all—the pivots, to-go orders, rearranging the restaurant maybe a hundred times, Edgar hoarding blue corn like toilet paper—we got through it by leaning on the community we'd built. With the survival of our businesses on the line, we didn't retreat to our corners—we came together. That's when we formed like Voltron and the Taco Mafia was born.

EDGAR: Later immortalized on a PBS show of the same name, the Taco Mafia refers to the little crew Sara and I created with the owners of three other taquerias—Beto Robledo of Cuantos Tacos, Anthony Pratto and Xose Velasco of Discada, and Jerry Guerrero of Palo Seco—in an effort to, I don't know, not cry ourselves to sleep every night.

Back in the day, Austin must have been a cutthroat town, because when people heard we were doing collabs with nearby taquerias, eyebrows raised, like, Isn't that the competition? Nah. First of all, we can't compete with Beto's Mexico City–style tacos, the beef and pork pulled from the lard pooling in his choricera. Same goes for Jerry's birria and for the one-of-a-kind taquitos at Discada, a magical merging of Xose's Mexico City upbringing and his dad's roots in the northern state of Chihuahua. The resulting melty mélange of meats, slowly sizzled in a vessel that looks like a wok fused with a plow blade, couldn't be more different than our cauliflower tacos with romesco sauce. Plus, they're our besties.

We big-upped each other, we fund-raised for each other, we shared equipment, advice, and people. We got through the hardest times together. During the 2021 Texas Freeze, we rallied to collect water and food and cooked it, wearing headlamps and over camp stoves, for hundreds of our neighbors. During early pandemic days, we worked with Austin Mutual Aid and the Free Fridge Program to launch the city's pilot community fridge that has fed thousands.

As we write this, we're still kicking, just out here trying to make it to the age of Sam's Barbecue. Every day, we wake up in Austin, in America, and we think about the guests we've seen grow up in front of our eyes. We've even seen some through dating to marriage to watching their babies coat themselves in duck-fat refried beans. We think about our grandparents and parents and how what they did was so much harder and came with no write-ups or awards or recognition of any sort. Every morning, we wonder, "What's broken today that I gotta fix?" The answer is always something, and eagerly if not always cheerily, we get to it.

FRIENDLY'S CAFE AND FLOUR TORTILLAS

The Iranian food I grew up eating occasionally finds its way onto the menu at Nixta. But for the most part, the food is all Edgar. Every so often, though, I stage a Persian takeover and resurrect Friendly's, my baba's dearly departed cafe. Channeling my creative genius, I call this pop-up . . . Friendlys.

In the early '90s, just before he dropped out of his PhD program (he was one class shy), Baba the Restless opened his convenience store slash gas station slash cafe. Actually, it reminded me of one of the Mexican setups you might see in Austin or New York or Chicago or LA—a shop in the front, seats and a tiny kitchen in the back. My young siblings and I would hang around Friendly's, serving folks who came in for their burgers or carton of cigarettes. (For immigrant parents, there is no prohibition against child labor.) Gregarious Baba presided, his swag a blend of dad jokes and borderline inappropriate zingers.

At our Friendlys pop-up, we welcome people Sara-style. We channel Baba's restlessness and gumption to even do a restaurant within a restaurant in the first place as well as the mehmoonis (those abundant Iranian gatherings, full of food and the warmest welcome) orchestrated by Maman and the rest of my family. We serve the food I grew up eating: kuku sabzi, a frittata that's more herb than egg, which is served with Maman's saffron-marinated fish (see page 143). There's Zeytoon Parvardeh (page 171), olives with pomegranate molasses, crushed walnuts, and herbs, and Ameh Fourouz's carrot jam (page 128), but made with black carrots from the farmers' market, and paired with Noon Barbari (page 125) and whipped ricotta. We even offer the Persian omelets aka Omelette Irooni (page 130) that Baba occasionally added to his Friendly's menu as a special.

Soon after Baba opened Friendly's, he hired a kind woman a generation older than him named Mary Martinez. An Iranian and a Mexican running a restaurant together, who could even imagine? Mary became family to us, "adopting" Maman, who frankly was lonely and needed adopting, and hosting us every weekend at her home in rural Arkansas, a good half hour outside Springdale. We'd pull up and Maman would start honking to scare off the cows on their farm, but it would attract more of them, and they'd surround the car.

We survived, and it was a good thing, too. Because Mary was a fantastic cook. I still dream about her orange-hued rice that had a sweet, soft onion buried in the middle, the fiery habanero salsa that Grandpa Martinez (aka Mary's husband, Bob) loved, and her tortillas, which I used to watch her roll from a mixture of flour and Crisco. Edgar, avert your eyes—I'm Team Flour Tortilla. At least if it's Mary's. I loved the texture, tender and delicate and chewy, almost like the lavash Maman made.

Mary was from the state of Monterrey, in Northern Mexico. The climate there is better for wheat than corn, and flour tortillas reign. They're king in Texas, too. Compared to the history of corn tortillas, their history is pretty googoo-gaga. But they're just as delicious and just as Mexican.

This recipe isn't Mary's. It's Edgar's, made with our forever-surplus of flavorful fat leftover from our duck carnitas, but just as good with pork lard or vegetable shortening.

DUCK-FAT FLOUR TORTILLAS

Equipment: stand mixer

- 3 cups/390g all-purpose flour, plus more if necessary
- 2 teaspoons/14g Morton kosher salt
- ¾ teaspoon/1.75g baking powder
- ¼ cup plus 2 tablespoons/ 85g warm (120° to 125°F) duck fat or pork lard
- ¾ cup plus 2 tablespoons/ 200g hot water (180° to 190°F), plus more if necessary

Makes twelve 8-inch tortillas

In a stand mixer fitted with the dough hook, combine the flour, salt, and baking powder and mix on low speed for 20 seconds or so, just to mix it all together.

Still on low speed, pour in the hot duck fat in a thin, steady stream, then mix until the mixture resembles damp sand, 1 to 2 minutes, stopping to scrape the bowl once.

Still on low, slowly stream in the warm water, then increase to medium speed and mix until the dough is smooth and supple and pulls cleanly from the sides of the bowl, about 8 minutes. The dough should be slightly tacky but shouldn't stick to your fingers. If it's dry, mix in more hot water, a tablespoon at a time; if it's sticky, mix in flour a tablespoon at a time, up to 4 tablespoons.

Turn off the mixer. Shape the dough into a rough ball, put it in a bowl, and cover with plastic wrap or a damp towel. Let it rest at room temperature to relax the gluten and let the dough fully hydrate for 1 hour.

Divide the dough into 12 equal pieces (52 grams each, if you're a weigher; the size of a golf ball, if you're a golfer). Between your palms, roll each piece into a tight ball, put in on a tray in a single layer, and cover with a damp towel. Let it rest for 15 minutes more.

Heat a large dry cast-iron skillet, comal, or griddle over medium-high.

Meanwhile, on a lightly floured surface or between sheets of parchment paper, use a rolling pin to roll one of the balls into a translucent-thin, 8-inch round, occasionally rotating the tortillas 90 degrees for even rolling. Dust the pin and round with more flour as necessary. It's okay if it's not a perfect circle, but really thin is vital.

When the skillet is hot, carefully lay the round flat onto the surface and cook, flipping once, until lightly golden in spots and puffed, 30 to 45 seconds per side.

As they're cooked, transfer them to a clean kitchen towel or tortilla warmer, stacking as you go. They'll stay soft and warm for up to 20 minutes.

They're best eaten right away. (Keeps in the fridge for a few days. Before serving, give them 5 to 10 seconds per side in a hot skillet.)

MIGAS TACOS

Austin-Style Eggs 'n' Chips

Born in Mexico, migas tacos are now as Texan as cowboy boots and odious senators. Few breakfasts on earth have this effort-to-wow ratio. At their essence, they're just crispy tortillas tumbled with scrambled eggs and then tucked into soft tortillas. We gussy them up with our game-changing refried beans, a little chorizo, and tangy tomatillo salsa.

Like most simple dishes, they get better with the quality of ingredients. So, seek out some proper nixtamalized chips and tortillas for this one. And have everything ready to go before you start the migas. You want to serve them right away, so the crunchy tortillas don't sog out.

12 corn tortillas

MIGAS

- 4 ounces fresh Mexican chorizo, casings removed
- 8 eggs, lightly beaten
- 1½ cups roughly crumbled tortilla chips or homemade Tostadas (page 39)
- Morton kosher salt

TACOS

- 1½ cups Duck-Fat Refried Beans (page 241), warmed
- Salsa Cruda (page 90) or Salsa de Habanero (page 92)
- Finely crumbled queso fresco
- Chopped cilantro
- 1 large Hass avocado, sliced, or Avocado Crema (page 89)
- Freshly ground black pepper
- Lime wedges, for squeezing

Makes 12 tacos

Warm and hold the tortillas (see how on page 38) before you start.

MAKE THE MIGAS: Put the chorizo in a large nonstick skillet, set over medium-high heat, and cook, breaking up the clumps, until cooked through and lightly browned, 3 to 4 minutes.

Remove the skillet from the heat, add the eggs, and cook, stirring frequently, until they're mostly cooked but still a little liquidy, about 2 minutes. If necessary for the eggs to cook, pop the skillet back over low heat.

Off the heat again, add the chips and a nice pinch of salt and stir for about 1 minute more, breaking up any large hunks of chips, until the eggs are cooked and the chips still have some crunch. Season with salt to taste.

ASSEMBLE THE TACOS: Have everyone spoon beans onto the tortillas, then top with the egg mixture and garnish with the salsa, queso fresco, cilantro, and avocado. Finish with some pepper and eat right away with the lime wedges.

SOFT SCRAMBLE 'N' RACLETTE TOSTADAS

Our guy Edgar isn't just some Mexican off the street, okay? He's put in time at *sophisticated* kitchens—you know, ones where they chop carrots really small and "mount" things with so much butter. Here, his lowly heritage converges with his venerable French training to give us the best cheese eggs ever—the softest of scrambles blanketed with gooey melted raclette, perched on a tostada as crisp as a tuile, and dribbled with dusky, aromatic, exceedingly sophisticated salsa macha.

8 tablespoons (4 ounces/ 1 stick) cold unsalted butter, cubed
8 eggs, lightly beaten
¼ cup thinly sliced chives, plus more for serving
1 teaspoon Morton kosher salt
Freshly ground black pepper
4 tostadas, store-bought or homemade (see page 39)
6 ounces raclette cheese (rind removed), sliced
Salsa macha, store-bought or homemade (see page 91), for serving
Flaky sea salt

Makes 4 tostadas

Move an oven rack to the top position and preheat the broiler.

Add about 7 tablespoons of the butter to a large nonstick skillet, set it over medium-high heat, and let it melt completely.

Lower the heat to medium. Add the eggs and cook, stirring constantly with a silicone spatula and moving the skillet on and off the heat every 20 seconds or so, until the eggs are just thickened, creamy, and small curds begin to form, about 4 minutes. Remove from the heat.

Fold in the chives, salt, and pepper to taste. Add the remaining 1 tablespoon butter and gently stir for 1 minute, until fully incorporated.

Arrange the tostadas on a large sheet pan, top with the eggs, and add a single layer of raclette slices to each tostada. Broil on the top rack just until the raclette is melty, 1 to 2 minutes.

Top with salsa macha, more chives, and flaky sea salt. Serve right away.

MASA PANCAKES

What began as an experiment has now become the only way we make pancakes. Incorporating masa into a classic batter takes just a little extra effort but adds a really nice earthy flavor and gives the exterior a delightfully crispy texture. These are primo pancakes whether you go full gluten-free or use regular all-purpose flour.

BATTER

- ⅔ cup masa harina, preferably heirloom corn
- ½ cup hot water
- 2 eggs
- 2 tablespoons sugar
- 5 tablespoons (2½ ounces) unsalted butter, cut into several pieces
- 1¼ cups buttermilk
- ¾ cup all-purpose gluten-free flour
- 2 tablespoons finely ground cornmeal
- ½ teaspoon baking powder
- ½ teaspoon baking soda
- ¼ teaspoon Morton kosher salt

FOR COOKING AND SERVING

- Unsalted butter
- Pure maple syrup

Serves 4

MAKE THE BATTER: In a medium bowl, combine the masa harina and hot water and use a flexible spatula to stir and scrape until smooth with no dry spots. Cover and set aside to cool, about 30 minutes.

Add the eggs and sugar to the bowl and use a handheld electric mixer or a whisk to mix until smooth (no lumps!), 1 to 2 minutes.

Melt the butter in a small pot over medium heat (or microwave it in a medium bowl), then stir in the buttermilk and cook (or microwave) until just warm to the touch. Add half of the buttermilk mixture to the bowl with the masa, stir until smooth, then add the rest of the buttermilk mixture and stir until smooth.

In a large bowl, whisk together the flour, cornmeal, baking powder, baking soda, and salt. Add the masa mixture to the bowl with the flour and mix until smooth with no dry spots.

COOK THE PANCAKES: Heat a large griddle or nonstick skillet over medium for a few minutes. When a drop of water sizzles and evaporates on contact, you're ready to roll.

Generously butter the griddle and let it froth. Scoop on ¼ cup of batter per pancake and cook in batches until bubbles form on the surface and the undersides are golden brown, about 3 minutes. Flip and cook until golden brown on the second side, about 2 minutes more.

Transfer the pancakes to plates or to a sheet pan in a very low oven to keep warm while you make the rest, adding more butter to the griddle between batches.

Serve topped with butter and maple syrup.

CUCUMBER SALAD WITH SALSA MACHA AND JAPANESE PEANUTS

This riff on Chinese cucumber salad is the kind of dish you throw together without much effort and then crave for days afterward. We briefly salt and drain the cukes to concentrate their flavor, then hit them with a dressing made with salsa macha, the Mexican counterpart to chili crisp. Crunchy Japanese peanuts (snacky Mexican fusion at its finest) and black sesame seeds add a little texture and color. It's not quite Mexican, not quite Chinese. It lives somewhere between the lines, which is where the best food often does.

DRESSING

- ½ cup salsa macha, store-bought or homemade (see page 91)
- 2 tablespoons toasted sesame oil
- 2 tablespoons demerara or granulated sugar
- 2 tablespoons unseasoned rice vinegar
- 1 garlic clove, peeled but whole

SALAD

- 2 pounds Persian (mini) cucumbers, ends trimmed
- 1 tablespoon Morton kosher salt, plus more to taste
- 1 small watermelon radish, quartered and very thinly sliced (on a mandoline)
- ½ cup cacahuates japoneses (Japanese-style peanuts; see Note), chopped
- 1 pint cherry tomatoes, halved lengthwise
- 1 tablespoon toasted black sesame seeds

Serves 4 to 6

MAKE THE DRESSING: In a blender, combine the salsa macha, sesame oil, sugar, vinegar, and garlic and blend on high until smooth and creamy, about 2 minutes. (At this point, you can refrigerate the dressing for up to 2 weeks.)

MAKE THE SALAD: Halve the cukes lengthwise, then cut them on the diagonal into slices ½ inch thick. In a large bowl, combine the cukes and the salt, toss well, and refrigerate, covered, for 1 hour.

Meanwhile, put the radish slices in a bowl of ice water and set aside for at least 20 minutes to crisp them up. Drain and pat the radish slices dry. Drain the cukes as well.

In a large serving bowl, combine the cold cukes, half the peanuts, and ¼ cup of the dressing (or more to taste) and toss well. Season to taste with salt.

Top with the radishes, tomatoes, remaining peanuts, and sesame seeds. Serve right away.

NOTE: Cacahuates japoneses (or Japanese peanuts) are a snacky peanut product invented in Mexico by Japanese immigrant Yoshigei Nakatani during the 1940s. The peanuts are encased in an extra-crunchy savory-sweet shell flavored with soy sauce, citric acid, and MSG, baby.

ELOTE-STYLE CORN RIBS

Our riff on elotes remixes the Mexican street-food classic—mayo-slathered, cheese-coated corn on the cob—with the corn rib. One of the few viral food trends ever to produce something worth making, these pretty, nibble-able curls of sweet corn are fun to serve and easy to make. Smoky chipotle mayo doubles down on the barbecue rib vibes.

Equipment: smoker or charcoal grill

- 4 large ears yellow sweet corn, shucked
- 8 tablespoons (4 ounces/1 stick) unsalted butter, melted
- ½ cup Chipotle Mayo (page 239)
- ¾ cup finely crumbled queso fresco
- 1 tablespoon thinly sliced chives
- Chopped cilantro, for serving
- 1 juicy lime, for squeezing
- 1½ teaspoons fine gochugaru (Korean chile powder) or Tajín

Serves 4 to 6

Prepare a smoker with mesquite to cook at 225°F. (Or grill nice and slow with charcoal and maybe with some mesquite chips.)

Cut the ears of corn into ribs (see Note). Drizzle the corn ribs with the melted butter and toss to coat.

Smoke the corn ribs for 1 hour, so they can absorb some nice smoky flavor. (Or grill until they curl and turn a nice deep yellow color, about 5 minutes.)

Transfer the corn ribs to a large bowl. Add the chipotle mayo, half the queso fresco, the chives, and most of the cilantro and tossy tossy.

We stack them on a serving plate log cabin–style, but you do you. Hit them with lime juice, the remaining cheese and cilantro, and the gochugaru. Serve right away.

NOTE: Done wrong, cutting corn cobs into riblets is the hardest thing you'll ever do. Done right, it's . . . easier but still a bit of a workout, so skip arms that week, y'all: Break or cut each ear in half crosswise. One by one, lay the pieces flat on a cutting board and use a sharp, sturdy bread knife to half them lengthwise, then halve them lengthwise again.

MASA-FRIED SPRING ONIONS

The inspo for the party snack is part Mexico, part Outback Steakhouse. At taquerias, I love to order a tangle of cebollitas, the charred slim onions, tender green stalks and all, that are griddled alongside whatever meats are on offer. The only thing that could make these better is crunch, kinda like the onions bloomin' in the fryer at everyone's favorite right-off-the-freeway steakhouse. Masa and vodka make the batter insanely light and crisp, and smoky chipotle mayo is a major upgrade to the chain-restaurant dip.

Equipment: deep-fry thermometer

- 1 pound (about 15) spring onions (see Note)
- Canola or another neutral oil, for deep-frying
- ⅔ cup masa harina, preferably heirloom corn
- 10½ tablespoons cornstarch, plus more as needed
- ½ teaspoon Morton kosher salt, plus more for finishing
- 1 egg white
- ½ cup plus 1 tablespoon sparkling water, very cold
- ½ cup ice-cold vodka
- Lime wedges, for squeezing
- Chipotle Mayo (page 239), for serving

Serves 4 to 6

Clean and trim the spring onions, leaving about 3 inches of the stalks attached. If the bulbs are any larger than 3 inches, quarter them lengthwise (through the stalk). If they're larger than 2 inches, halve them.

Stick a medium mixing bowl in the freezer for at least 15 minutes. Set a wire rack in a sheet pan and keep them near the stove. Pour 3 inches oil into a deep heavy-bottomed pot and heat over medium-high to 350°F.

Meanwhile, into a small mixing bowl, sift the masa harina, cornstarch, and salt and mixy mixy. Set aside. In another small mixing bowl, whisk the egg whites vigorously until bubbly and roughly doubled in volume, 30 seconds to 1 minute. Set aside.

Take out the frozen bowl, add the sparkling water and vodka, and mixy mixy. About a tablespoon at a time, add the masa harina mixture to the liquid mixture, whisking to incorporate so no dry spots remain. Add the eggs and mix until smooth. If necessary, gradually add more cornstarch so the mixture is a little thicker than pancake batter. If I were you, I'd add the bowl to another bowl of very icy water to keep it extra cold.

When the oil is ready, fry in several batches like so: Submerge a few onions at a time in the batter, let any excess drip off, and one by one transfer them to the hot oil. Fry until golden and crisp, stirring once after 30 seconds or so just to make sure they don't stick together, 2 to 3 minutes.

As they're fried, transfer to the wire rack and immediately season with a pinch of salt. Let the oil return to temp before frying the next batch.

Serve hot with lime wedges and chipotle mayo for dipping.

NOTE: Spring onions are young onions with tender green stalks and slightly chubby bulbs—basically, like scallions with a little gut. Seek them out at the farmers' market during the spring and summer or at Mexican markets year-round, where they're sold as cebollinas, cebollitas, or cebollas cambray.

RED LENTIL SOUP WITH CHOCHOYOTES

Mexican Masa Dumplings

Chochoyotes are dimpled little pucks of masa, like light, tender nixtamalized corn dumplings—in the American South sense of the word. They tend to show up in soups and brothy stews, like mole de olla. (They can also be fried up crispy and tucked in a tortilla, for a little masa-on-masa action.) At Nixta, sometimes we rock chochoyotes in a silky lentil soup, enriched with sweet potatoes, coconut milk, and garam masala, then topped with crema, cilantro, and salsa macha. It's a little South Asian, a little Mexican, and a lot delicious.

SOUP

- 6 tablespoons extra-virgin olive oil
- 1 medium sweet potato, peeled and cut into ½-inch dice
- 1 small white onion, cut into ½-inch dice
- 2 medium jalapeño chiles (seeded if you scared), chopped
- 5 garlic cloves, roughly chopped
- 1 tablespoon garam masala
- 1 tablespoon ground ginger
- 1 tablespoon chopped sage
- 1½ teaspoons ancho chile powder
- 1¾ cups red lentils
- 8 cups water
- One 13.5-ounce can full-fat coconut milk
- 1 teaspoon Maggi seasoning
- 1½ tablespoons Morton kosher salt

CHOCHOYOTES

- 1 cup masa harina, preferably heirloom corn, plus more if needed
- ½ teaspoon Morton kosher salt, plus more for boiling
- 1 cup warm water (about 100°F), plus more if needed
- ½ cup neutral oil, such as grapeseed or canola

FOR SERVING

- Salsa macha, store-bought or homemade (see page 91)
- Mexican crema
- Cilantro sprigs
- Lime wedges

Serves 4 to 6

MAKE THE SOUP: Heat the olive oil in a large Dutch oven or heavy pot over medium until it shimmers. Add the sweet potato and cook, stirring, until it begins to soften, 6 to 8 minutes. Stir in the onion, jalapeños, and garlic and cook until the onions are translucent, 6 to 8 minutes more.

Add the garam masala, ginger, sage, and ancho powder and stir until fragrant, about 2 minutes. Add the red lentils and stir to coat in the fun stuff. Pour in the water, coconut milk, and Maggi and bring to a boil. Lower the heat to cook at a moderate simmer, uncovered, until the lentils break down and thicken up the soup, 25 to 30 minutes. Stir in the salt.

Blend the soup—an immersion blender is easiest, but batches in a stand blender is cool—until smooth and velvety. Keep warm on low heat until ready to serve.

MAKE THE CHOCHOYOTES: In a medium bowl, combine the masa harina and salt, then pour in the warm water. Use your hands to bring the mixture together into a dough with no masa harina stuck to the sides.

Knead until no dry patches remain. The dough should feel moist but not sticky, almost like Play-Doh, leaving a light film of residual moisture on your hands. If it's sticky, gradually mix in more masa harina. If it's dry, gradually mix in more warm water. Cover with a damp towel and let rest for 10 minutes.

Roll the dough into 1-inch balls and press with your thumb to make a divot in the center of each one so they're like little cups—this helps them cook evenly and grab onto the soup. As you make them, transfer to a plate.

In a large skillet, heat the oil over medium heat until it shimmers. Working in two batches, cook the chochoyotes, flipping once, until very lightly colored on both sides, 2 to 3 minutes per side. Transfer them to a plate or tray, leaving the oil behind.

TO SERVE: Ladle the soup into bowls. Add the chochoyotes, then drizzle generously with salsa macha and crema, and top with cilantro. Serve with lime wedges.

SMASH BURGERS AL PASTOR

One summer in Mexico as a kid, I refused to eat Mexican food. So, I ate a lot of burgers. What's more American than that? Ironically, the burgers I ended up eating were actually extremely Mexican. They were made on the griddles of streetside stands with crazy names (Batman Burger, Dragonball-Z Burger!). They were topped with stuff like refried beans, charred chiles, ham, chorizo, or lime mayo.

My people really know how to take food from somewhere else and make it ours. It's in that glorious tradition that we riff on the classic smash burger, subbing out the beef for ground pork that's been marinated like al pastor—the pork rotating on spits like Mexican shawarma. Caramelized pineapple and tomatillo salsa on top give you taco al pastor vibes, just nestled on buns instead of tortillas.

PATTIES

- ½ medium white onion, roughly chopped
- 4 garlic cloves, peeled but whole
- ¼ cup ancho chile powder
- 2 tablespoons apple cider vinegar
- 2 tablespoons vegetarian pineapple fish sauce (see Note), or 1½ tablespoons fish sauce
- 1½ tablespoons achiote paste, such as El Yucateco
- ½ teaspoon dried oregano, preferably Mexican
- ¼ teaspoon ground cinnamon, preferably Mexican canela
- ⅛ teaspoon freshly ground black pepper
- ⅛ teaspoon ground cumin
- 1 pound ground pork

BURGERS

- 1 medium Hass avocado
- 1⅓ cups Salsa Cruda (page 90)
- 6 rings (about ¼ inch thick) cored, peeled ripe pineapple
- 6 large potato buns, such as Big Marty's
- ½ medium white onion, very thinly sliced (on a mandoline)
- 12 slices pepper Jack cheese
- Drained dill pickle chips

Makes 6 double burgers

MAKE THE PATTIES: In a blender, combine everything but the pork and blend until smooth, scraping down the sides and gradually adding water if necessary to help the mixture blend.

In a medium bowl, combine the pork and blended mixture, mix really well with your hands, and refrigerate, covered, for at least 12 or up to 24 hours.

COOK THE BURGERS: Halve and pit the avocado, and scoop the avocado flesh into a blender. Add the salsa and blend until smooth and creamy. Set aside.

Preheat the broiler. Arrange the pineapple slices on a large sheet pan and broil a few inches from the broiler, flipping once, until deeply caramelized on both sides, 8 to 12 minutes total. Set aside.

Lightly toast the potato rolls.

Preheat a cast-iron griddle or skillet over medium-high heat for 5 minutes.

Divide the marinated pork into 12 equal portions (54 grams each) and shape into balls. Working in batches, add the pork balls to the griddle with a few inches of space between them. Top each ball with a big pinch of the onion slices and give them a light press so they adhere.

Cook undisturbed for 1 minute.

Lay a piece of parchment paper over one of the balls and use a grill press, large can, or bottom of a small skillet to evenly and firmly press to make a super-thin patty. Repeat with the other balls on the griddle.

Cook until the bottoms are deep golden brown, 2 to 3 minutes, then flip the patties and immediately add a slice of pepper Jack cheese to each one. Cook until the cheese melts, about 2 minutes more.

Spread the avocado/salsa mixture generously on both bun halves. Top the bottom buns with 2 of the pork patties, then a pineapple ring and some dill pickle chips. Close them up and serve while you cook the rest.

NOTE: Known as nuoc mam chay in Vietnamese, this pineapple-based sauce is a fermented product meant to match the umami flavor of fish sauce. I prefer it in this recipe for the way that its tropical vibes play with the pineapple in the dish. Regular fish sauce is fine, too—because it's more intense, you'd just use a little less.

SPACE GLIZZIES

Crispy Dawgs

We probably wouldn't have even heard of this one if it weren't for Luna, former Nixta team member. In San Antonio, it's called the Crispy Dog. At Nixta, it goes by the Space Glizzy. We're basically talking about a Tex-Mex corn dog, just with a different sort of corn. Instead of dipping a big beef frank in cornmeal batter, you roll a tortilla around that glizzy—while you're at it, maybe you also slide in a slice of American cheese—and fry it until crisp. It's a goddamn hot dog flauta! Ketchup, mustard, and tomatillo relish are the condiments of choice—not ranch, Sara!

Equipment: 12 toothpicks, deep-fry thermometer

THE RELISH

2 medium tomatillos, husked, washed, and finely chopped
½ serrano chile, seeded and finely minced
¼ cup very finely chopped white onion
2 tablespoons finely chopped cilantro
¼ teaspoon Morton kosher salt, plus more to taste
Finely grated zest of 1 lime
1 tablespoon fresh lime juice

THE GLIZZIES

6 corn tortillas
6 slices American cheese (we like Boar's Head)
6 hot dogs, preferably Hebrew National, patted dry
Neutral oil, such as grapeseed or canola, for shallow-frying

FOR SERVING

Ketchup
Yellow mustard
Ranch dressing (Team Sara) or nothing else (Team Edgar)
¼ cup Puffed Amaranth (optional; page 240)

Makes 6 glizzies

MAKE THE RELISH: In a small bowl, combine the tomatillos, chile, onion, cilantro, salt, lime zest, and lime juice. Stir well, season to taste, and set aside. (At this point, you can refrigerate the relish for up to 1 day.)

COOK THE GLIZZIES: In a hot dry medium skillet, heat the tortillas one at a time until pliable, about 20 seconds per side. Set them aside. While they're still warm, lay a slice of cheese on each tortilla, add a dog in the middle, and roll the tortilla tightly around the dog, securing it with a toothpick at each end.

Line a plate with paper towels and keep them near the stove. Pour 1 inch of oil into the skillet and bring to 350°F over medium-high heat. Lower the heat to medium, then carefully add 3 of the dogs, one at a time. Fry, turning occasionally with tongs, until golden and crispy, about 3 minutes. Transfer to the paper towels to absorb the excess oil. Repeat with the remaining dogs.

TO SERVE: Top the dogs with squiggles of ketchup mustard, and ranch, a spoonful of tomatillo relish, and a sprinkle of the puffed amaranth.

ROWDY ABOUT RANCH

The most American (or maybe, Arkansan) thing about Sara is her unbridled love of ranch dressing. It's her favorite condiment by a mile. Mayo? Nah. Ketchup? GTFOH. Despite or perhaps because of this affection, you won't find a recipe for ranch here, because Sara says you just can't beat a bottle of Hidden Valley. She recommends it for these glizzies as well as for Kotlet (page 136), fish tacos (see page 62), and literally everything else. Hers is a profound love, and more than a little concerning.

BEET "TARTARE" TOSTADAS

A pile of cubed roasted beets tossed with salsa macha and mayo really does resemble beef tartare. A bite, however, reveals something even more delicious. We brighten the sweet, smoky, earthy jumble with horseradish and lime, then serve it on crispy tortillas slathered with avocado crema.

Chopping the beets into tiny dice amplifies the tartare effect, but you do you. Using vegan mayo lets everyone partake, and a good plant-based one, like Duke's, lets even omnivores enjoy.

BEET "TARTARE"

- 1 pound trimmed red beets
- 1 tablespoon extra-virgin olive oil
- 1 teaspoon Morton kosher salt, plus more to taste
- ¼ cup red wine vinegar
- ¼ cup vegan mayo or regular mayo (Duke's!)
- 2½ tablespoons salsa macha, store-bought or homemade (see page 91)
- ¼ cup finely chopped cilantro
- 2 tablespoons finely chopped shallots
- 1 generous tablespoon finely chopped capers

TOSTADAS

- 3 cups Avocado Crema (page 89)
- 12 tostadas, store-bought or homemade (see page 39)
- Knob of horseradish, top 2 inches or so peeled
- 2 limes
- Micro radish greens
- Best olive oil you've got
- Flaky sea salt

Makes 12 tostadas

MAKE THE BEET "TARTARE": Preheat the oven to 400°F.

Arrange the beets in a medium baking dish or pie plate in a single layer. Add the oil and ½ teaspoon of the salt and toss to coat well. Pour in about ¼ inch water, then the vinegar, and cover tightly with foil.

Roast until a sharp knife inserted into the center of the beets meets with no resistance, 45 minutes to 1 hour 15 minutes (depending on size). Discard any remaining liquid and let the beets cool to the touch.

Rub the beets to remove the skins (wear gloves if you don't want Grimace fingers). Cut the beets into ⅛-inch dice (or larger, if you're feeling lazy) and put them in a bowl. Add the mayo, salsa macha, cilantro, shallots, capers, and remaining ½ teaspoon salt. Mixy mixy, then season to taste with more salt.

MAKE THE TOSTADAS: Spread (or pipe!) about ¼ cup avocado crema onto the center of each tostada. Dollop (or quenelle!) the beet "tartare" onto the crema, about ¼ cup per tostada.

Microplane on some horseradish and lime zest, add a nice nest of microgreens, then finish with a drizzle of olive oil and flaky salt. Cut the limes into wedges and serve alongside.

KALE CAESAR TOSTADAS

Salad loves crunch. Tostadas *are* crunch. So, try your next salad on a tortilla, especially if it's a Caesar, which after all was born in Tijuana. Dino kale stands up to the creamy dressing, our spiced-up take on the classic, and a sprinkle of buttery bread crumbs doubles down on the crunch.

DRESSING

- ¼ cup fresh lemon juice (1 to 2 lemons)
- 3 tablespoons red wine vinegar
- 2 tablespoons Mexican crema or sour cream
- 2 tablespoons salsa macha, store-bought or homemade (see page 91)
- 1 tablespoon balsamic vinegar
- 1 tablespoon Worcestershire sauce
- 2 teaspoons Dijon mustard
- 1½ teaspoons hot sauce, homemade (see page 239) or sriracha
- 1½ teaspoons Morton kosher salt, plus more to taste
- 1½ teaspoons freshly ground black pepper, plus more to taste
- 1 garlic clove, grated
- 4 egg yolks
- 2 oil-packed anchovy fillets, drained
- 1½ cups extra-virgin olive oil
- ½ cup finely grated Parmigiano-Reggiano cheese
- ¼ cup minced shallot

BREAD CRUMBS

- 8 tablespoons (4 ounces/1 stick) unsalted butter, cut into chunks
- ¼ cup extra-virgin olive oil
- 2 cups panko bread crumbs
- 2 teaspoons finely chopped oregano or ¾ teaspoon dried
- 3 garlic cloves, finely minced or grated
- ½ teaspoon Morton kosher salt

TOSTADAS

- 2 bunches of lacinato/Tuscan/dino kale (1½ pounds total)
- Kosher salt and freshly ground black pepper
- 3 medium Hass avocados
- 12 tostadas, store-bought or homemade (see page 39)
- Parmigiano-Reggiano cheese, for serving

Makes 12 tostadas

MAKE THE DRESSING: In a food processor, combine all the stuff in the ingredient list up to the olive oil and process until smoothish. With the machine running, slowly drizzle in the oil. Scrape the dressing into a medium bowl and stir in the Parmigiano and shallot. Season with more salt and pepper as needed. (At this point, you can refrigerate the dressing for up to 5 days.)

MAKE THE BREAD CRUMBS: Line a sheet pan with paper towels and keep it near the stove. In a large skillet, combine the butter and olive oil and set over medium heat until frothy. Add the panko, adjust the heat to medium-low, and cook, stirring, until crispy and golden, 8 to 10 minutes. Remove the pan from the heat, stir in the oregano and garlic, and stir in the salt. Transfer to the paper towels to drain.

MAKE THE TOSTADAS: Remove the kale stems and very thinly slice the leaves. You'll have 6 to 7 cups. In a large bowl, toss the kale with ¾ cup of the dressing (or more to taste) and massage with your hands to evenly coat. Season with salt and pepper to taste.

Pit and peel the avocados, then cut them into long thin slices. Top the tostadas with the avocado slices, then the kale salad, then the bread crumbs. Microplane on so much Parm and serve.

8-29
OILS

TUNA TOSTADAS

When we get our hands on top-notch tuna, we marinate thin slices in tamari and citrus, then lay them on tostadas. A drizzle of chipotle mayo and a sprinkle of furikake (the umami-packed Japanese shake-on seasoning) gives it sushi-bar-in-Mexico-City vibes.

TUNA

- 1½ pounds sushi-grade yellowfin tuna
- 1½ cups tamari or Japanese soy sauce
- Finely grated zest of 3 limes
- 6 tablespoons fresh lime juice
- Finely grated zest of 2 oranges
- 3 tablespoons freshly squeezed orange juice

TOSTADAS

- ½ cup Chipotle Mayo (page 239) or more to taste
- 2 large Hass avocados
- 8 tostadas, store-bought or homemade (see page 39)
- Furikake, preferably nori komi
- Micro cilantro or chopped cilantro
- Flaky sea salt
- Best olive oil you've got
- Lime wedges

Makes 8 tostadas

PREPARE THE TUNA: Line a plate or sheet pan with parchment paper. Arrange the tuna in a single layer on the parchment and freeze for 30 minutes to make slicing easier.

While it's in the freezer, in a narrow container that'll also fit the sliced tuna comfortably, combine the tamari, lime zest, lime juice, orange zest, and orange juice and whisk well. Set aside.

ASSEMBLE THE TOSTADAS: Put the chipotle mayo in a resealable bag (or use a squeeze bottle). Set aside.

Pit and peel the avocados, then cut them into long thin slices. Top each tostada with 3 or 4 slices of the avocado.

Cut the tuna against the grain into ⅛-inch-thick slices. Add the slices to the tamari mixture and toss well. Let marinate for 2 minutes, tossing again halfway through. Transfer the slices to paper towels to drain, discarding the marinade. Lay the tuna slices over the avocado. Edge to edge with tuna, baby.

Twist the resealable bag to force the mayo toward a corner, snip the corner, and zigzag it across each tostada. Sprinkle on some furikake, add a little nest of micro cilantro, then sprinkle with some flaky salt and lightly drizzle with olive oil.

Serve right away with lime wedges.

HAMACHI TOSTADAS

With tostadas as the canvas, your options are limitless. Take these stunners, which dip into Southeast Asian territory. Buttery slices of raw yellowtail get a quickie cure to firm and flavor them, then comes a brief soak in a sweet-savory vinaigrette made with lime, fish sauce, and piloncillo (Mexican unrefined cane sugar). A heap of fresh herbs, some slivered chile, and a shower of crunchy fried shallots complete the detour while avocado reminds you where your journey began.

HAMACHI

2 cups Morton kosher salt
1 cup sugar
¾ teaspoon ground chile pequín or chile de árbol
Finely grated zest of 1 orange
Finely grated zest of 1 lime
1 pound skinless yellowtail (hamachi) fillets

TOSTADAS

3 large Hass avocados
1 cup Piloncillo Dressing (page 240)
12 tostadas, store-bought or homemade (see page 39)
Flaky sea salt
Mixed herbs (cilantro, mint leaves, and/or Persian or Thai basil)
Store-bought fried shallots
1 Fresno chile, sliced as thin as possible
Best olive oil you've got
Lime wedges

Makes 12 tostadas

CURE THE HAMACHI: In a large bowl, mix together the salt, sugar, ground chile, orange zest, and lime zest. Add the hamachi and bury it in the cure, making sure it's well coated on all sides. Pop it in the fridge for 20 minutes to cure.

Rinse the hamachi under water to remove the cure and pat dry. (At this point, you can cover and refrigerate the fish for up to 1 day.)

MAKE THE TOSTADAS: Pit and peel the avocados, then cut them into long thin slices. Cut the hamachi against the grain into ⅛-inch-thick slices. Pop them in a clean bowl, add the dressing, and toss well. Let marinate for 1 minute, then transfer the slices to paper towels, reserving some marinade for drizzling.

Top each tostada with avocado slices, sprinkle with flaky sea salt, then lay on the hamachi. Garnish with the herbs, crispy shallots, and sliced chiles. Add a drizzle of olive oil, a drizzle of reserved marinade, and a sprinkle of flaky salt.

Serve right away with lime wedges.

9-1
Fish
9-1

WHITEFISH SALAD TOSTADAS

Inspired by our love for the Jewish deli, we scoop a generous pile of whitefish salad on a flat masa bagel with no hole. (Okay, fine, it's a tostada.) If you ask us, the smoked fish, amped up with smoky chipotle and pickled red onion, would kill at the seafood-centric tostada spots in Mexico, not to mention the sable-slingers in LA and New York.

Don't have salsa morita on hand? Use finely chopped chipotle peppers in adobo mixed with some of the sauciness in the can.

WHITEFISH SALAD

1 pound smoked whitefish, skin and bones removed
⅔ cup mayo (Duke's!)
⅓ cup finely diced white onion
3 tablespoons Salsa Morita (page 90), plus more to taste
2 teaspoons finely chopped dill
Juice of 1 lemon, plus more to taste
Kosher salt

TOSTADAS

10 tostadas, store-bought or homemade (see page 39)
1 cup Pickled Red Onions (page 93), drained well
1 cup mixed chopped dill, chives, and celery leaves
Nixta's Fresno Hot Sauce (page 239) or sriracha
Best olive oil you've got
Flaky sea salt
Lemon wedges

Makes 10 tostadas

MAKE THE WHITEFISH SALAD: Put the whitefish in a large bowl and use a fork to mix and mash it a bit as you look for and remove any lingering bones. Add the mayo, white onion, salsa, dill, and lemon juice and mix and mash to the fine texture of deli whitefish salad/tuna salad. Season to taste with salt, lemon juice, and salsa. Cover and refrigerate until chilled, at least 1 hour or up to 2 days.

ASSEMBLE THE TOSTADAS: Spread the whitefish salad evenly onto each tostada. Garnish with the pickled onions and mixed dill, chives, and celery leaves. Add a few dashes of hot sauce, a drizzle of olive oil, and a sprinkle of flaky salt.

Serve right away with the lemon wedges.

CARROT TOSTADAS

In Texas, we love us some smoke, and here we apply it to carrots for everyone's surprise fave. Pretty carrots get a heavy dose of salt and pepper, just like brisket, then turn all sweet, charred, and smoky on the grill. We lay them on a mattress of herby whipped cream cheese (the bedframe is a crispy tostada) and blanket them with herbs and carrot tops tossed with sweet-tart vinaigrette.

Equipment: stand mixer or handheld mixer, outdoor grill or grill pan

HERBY BIZNIZ

- 1 pound cream cheese, at room temp
- 3 tablespoons chopped cilantro
- 2 tablespoons chopped mint leaves
- ½ teaspoon Morton kosher salt
- ¼ teaspoon freshly ground black pepper

TOSTADAS

- 20 trimmed medium carrots (about 1¾ pounds total), scrubbed or peeled, tops reserved
- ¼ cup extra-virgin olive oil, plus a lil' drizzle
- 1 tablespoon Morton kosher salt, plus a big pinch
- 1 tablespoon freshly ground black pepper
- 2 tablespoons salsa macha, store-bought or homemade (see page 91), plus more for drizzling
- 1 cup packed cilantro leaves
- 1 cup packed mint leaves
- 1½ teaspoons red wine vinegar
- 1½ teaspoons date molasses or maple syrup, plus more for drizzling
- 12 tostadas, store-bought or homemade (see page 39)
- Puffed Amaranth (optional; page 240)

Makes 12 tostadas

MAKE THE HERBY BIZNIZ: In a stand mixer fitted with the whisk (or in a bowl with a handheld mixer), combine the cream cheese, cilantro, mint, salt, and pepper and beat on medium speed until well mixed and fluffy, 1 to 2 minutes. Set aside or transfer to a resealable bag for piping, if you're feeling fancy. (At this point, you can refrigerate the mixture for up to 3 days. Let it come to room temp before using.)

MAKE THE TOSTADAS: Preheat a grill (or a grill pan) to cook with high heat. In a large bowl, toss the carrots with the olive oil, salt, and pepper to coat well. Lay the carrots on the grill, lower the heat to medium (or medium-high for the grill pan), and cook, uncovered, turning often, until dark brown with spots of char and tender-crisp, 12 to 18 minutes, depending on the thickness of the carrots.

Transfer to a cutting board to cool slightly. Thinly slice the carrots on a harsh diagonal. Transfer to a large bowl, add the salsa macha, and toss to coat. Set aside to marinate, 5 to 10 minutes, while you finish up.

Fill a medium bowl with ice water. Pick a cup or so of the frilly carrot tops from the stems, add them to the ice water, and let them hang out for a few minutes to get perky. Drain and pat them dry.

In another bowl, toss together the carrot tops, cilantro, mint, vinegar, molasses, a drizzle of olive oil, and a big pinch of salt.

Spread (or pipe) the herby business on each tostada. Top with the carrots, garnish with carrot top mixture, and drizzle with additional salsa macha and date molasses to taste. Top with the puffed amaranth, and serve right away.

CAULIFLOWER TACOS

At Nixta, we wanted some of our tacos to have seasonal vibes, so for our first fall, we hit the market for some dope cauliflower and put it on the menu. People loved it so much that the fleeting special became a permanent fixture. The key is to give that cauliflower a really hard char, in the oven or on the grill, which brings out some meaty notes along with the vegetable's typically sweet, nutty qualities.

Tangy, smoky romesco sauces shit up. It has a lot in common with salsa—it's a punchy, salty coarse puree of charred vegetables, after all. We tweak the classic by adding cilantro and swapping out the traditional almonds for rich, toasty pecans for a little Texas pride.

ROMESCO SALSA

- 3 medium red bell peppers
- 1 medium Roma or plum tomato
- ½ cup extra-virgin olive oil
- 3 tablespoons fresh lemon juice
- 2 tablespoons red wine vinegar
- 1 tablespoon Morton kosher salt
- 1 tablespoon smoked paprika
- ½ teaspoon cayenne pepper
- ¾ cup raw pecans
- 3 large garlic cloves, peeled but whole
- 1 cup roughly chopped cilantro

TACOS

- 6 tablespoons pine nuts
- 12 to 15 corn tortillas
- ¼ cup neutral oil, such as grapeseed or canola
- 8 cups (1½-inch) cauliflower florets (from 1 large head)
- 2 teaspoons Morton kosher salt, plus more to taste
- Crumbled queso fresco
- Chopped cilantro
- Best olive oil you've got
- Flaky sea salt
- Lime wedges

Serves 4 to 6

MAKE THE ROMESCO SALSA: Preheat the oven broiler with a rack 3 to 4 inches from the heat. Put the bell peppers and tomato on a large sheet pan with some space between them and broil, turning them occasionally to make sure they get blistered and charred all over, 15 to 20 minutes.

Transfer the peppers to a large bowl, cover tightly, and let sit for 30 minutes to make them easier to peel. Pull off and discard the stems from the peppers. Halve the peppers, remove the seeds and veins, and use your fingers or a paring knife to remove the skin (no rinsing, though!). Cut out the core of the tomato.

In a blender, combine the peppers and tomato. Add the oil, lemon juice, vinegar, salt, smoked paprika, cayenne, pecans, garlic, and cilantro and blend on high until smooth, about 2 minutes. (At this point, you can refrigerate the romesco salsa for up to 3 days.)

MAKE THE TACOS: Preheat the oven to 350°F.

Spread the pine nuts on a small sheet pan and toast, shaking the pan occasionally, until deep golden, 8 to 10 minutes.

Warm and hold the tortillas (see how on page 38).

To grill, prepare a grill to cook with medium heat. In a big bowl, toss together the oil, cauliflower, and salt. To cook on the stovetop, heat a large cast-iron skillet over medium heat, add half the oil, and let it shimmer. Add half the cauliflower in a single layer, season with half the salt, and set something clean and heavy (a pot or another skillet) on the cauliflower to weight it down. Cook with the weight, flipping the florets once, until deep golden brown (almost black in spots) and tender with a nice bite, 4 to 5 minutes per side. Transfer to a plate and spread them out in a single layer. Add the remaining oil and cook the remaining cauliflower the same way. Season to taste with more salt.

Serve the cauliflower with the tortillas, romesco salsa, queso fresco, and cilantro for making tacos. Finish each with a drizzle of olive oil, a sprinkle of flaky sea salt, and a squeeze of lime juice.

BEAN AND CHEESE TACOS

This is one of those, "How can something this simple be this good?" dishes. All it is: a soft steamy tortilla, a generous swipe of our duck-fat refried beans, and a thick slice of griddled panela cheese (Mexico's answer to Halloumi). But my lord! And to think it began as baby food.

In our kitchen POS system, we had a button labeled "Beanie Baby" that put in an order for this taco. Guests had remarked that the menu didn't have an option for kids, so we gave them one and they got it all over their cute little faces. For these beanie babies, we leave off the salsa. But for the adults who have become obsessed with the taco, we spoon on the sweet, smoky condiment, which is pure magic with that salty, buttery cheese.

If you have any leftover Avocado Crema (page 89) and/or cooked Mexican chorizo, try loading them, too.

4 cups Duck-Fat Refried Beans (page 241)
12 corn tortillas
Twelve ¼-inch-thick slabs queso panela (about ½ pound)
4 tablespoons (2 ounces/ ½ stick) unsalted butter
Salsa Morita (page 90), for serving

Makes 12 tacos

In a medium pot, heat up the beans over low heat. Gradually add enough water for a creamy-thick consistency.

Warm and hold the tortillas (see how on page 38).

Pat the panela slabs dry, so they don't splatter too much. Melt the butter in a medium skillet over medium heat until it bubbles. Working in batches to avoid overcrowding, sear the panela, flipping once, until deep golden brown on both sides, 4 to 6 minutes total. As they're done, transfer to a plate.

Spoon the beans in the center of each tortilla and spread a lil' bit. Top each with a panela slab, spoon on some salsa, and serve right away.

DUCK CARNITAS TACOS

This is the dish that keeps the lights on, by a mile the most popular thing on our menu. Classic carnitas (tender, crisp-edged pork) is already epic, so when duck gets involved, you know shit's going to be wild. We briefly infuse duck fat with aromatics like orange, garlic, and dried chiles, spike it with sweetened condensed milk and Coke (the magic behind modern-day carnitas), and let the duck legs gently bubble until the meat is as tender as a mother's embrace.

Crisped up in a pan, the duck is the tortilla topper that dreams are made of, especially with a little crisp vegetation and a stripe of zingy tomatillo salsa. And because the dish is a gift that keeps giving, you're also left with incredibly flavorful duck fat to use for refried beans (see page 241), making flour tortillas (page 189), and making your next round of duck carnitas, which will taste even better for it.

DUCK CARNITAS

- 6 duck legs (6 to 8 ounces each)
- 2 tablespoons Morton kosher salt
- 1 tablespoon freshly ground black pepper
- 8 cups duck fat
- One 12-ounce bottle Coke
- ¾ cup plus 2 tablespoons sweetened condensed milk
- 1 medium white onion, peeled and quartered
- 1 head garlic, halved horizontally
- 1 dried guajillo chile, stemmed but whole
- 1 dried ancho chile, stemmed but whole
- 1 orange, quartered
- 1 bay leaf

TACOS

- About ½ cup very thinly sliced white onions
- 1 or 2 small watermelon radishes, very thinly sliced
- 12 to 15 corn tortillas
- Handful of chopped cilantro
- Flaky sea salt
- Salsa Cruda (page 90) or Salsa de Habanero (page 92)

Makes 12 to 15 tacos

MAKE THE DUCK CARNITAS: Preheat the oven to 225°F.

Evenly season the duck legs on both sides with the salt and pepper. Heat a 6-quart Dutch oven over medium-high heat, add 1 tablespoon of the duck fat, and let it melt and shimmer. Working in two batches, add the duck legs skin-side down and cook, flipping once, until golden on both sides, 5 to 6 minutes per side. Transfer to a plate, leaving the fat in the pot.

Add the remaining duck fat to the pot along with the Coke, condensed milk, onion, garlic, guajillo, ancho, orange, and bay leaf and stir well. Lower the heat to medium, wait until the fat begins to bubble, and cook for 15 minutes more to let the flavors infuse the fat.

Add the duck legs to the Dutch oven in two layers so that they're submerged in the fat. Cover the pot, transfer to the oven, and cook, until the meat is falling off the bone, about 4 hours, rotating the pot halfway through. Let the duck cool completely in the fat.

Remove the duck legs. Strain the duck fat into a big bowl, discarding the solids. (At this point, you can submerge the whole duck legs in the fat and store in the fridge. The duck legs [which go great with Mole Rojo, page 87] keep for up to 1 week, and the fat keeps for up to 3 months. To remove the legs, gently warm the fat until it's liquid.)

MAKE THE TACOS: Pick off the meat and skin, discarding the bones, and give it a good chop.

Fill two medium bowls with ice water. Add the onion to one and the radishes to the other to crisp them up and remove some of their sharpness. Set aside while you finish the dish.

Warm and hold the tortillas (see how on page 38).

Heat a large skillet over medium, add ¼ cup of the reserved duck fat, and let it shimmer. Add the duck meat in a single layer and cook, without stirring, until crispy on the bottom and hot through, 3 to 4 minutes.

Drain and pat dry the onions and radishes. Serve the duck in the skillet with the tortillas, onions, radishes, cilantro, flaky salt, and salsa on the side for making tacos.

COCO RICO PALETAS

Coconut Ice Pops

Three forms of coconut team up to make this day-one banger. Dead simple to make, these paletas (ice pops) deliver so much rich, creamy coconut flavor, plus the crunchy coating of coconut chips.

Equipment: one 12-pop mold (3 ounces per pop), 12 ice pop sticks

- 2 cups heavy cream
- One 15-ounce can Coco López cream of coconut
- 7 tablespoons canned coconut milk, preferably Chaokoh
- 2½ cups untoasted unsweetened coconut chips

Makes 12 pops

In a blender, combine the heavy cream, cream of coconut, and coconut milk and blend for a minute or so, until you get thick heavy cream/crème fraîche vibes.

Pour the mixture directly into the molds and add the ice pop sticks. If the mold doesn't have a cover, make sure to cover it so you don't get freezer burn. (You might have a little mixture left over.) Freeze until fully frozen, at least 6 hours or up to 2 months.

Half an hour or so before you're ready to eat, preheat the oven to 350°F.

Spread the coconut chips on a large sheet pan and toast in the oven until golden, about 10 minutes. Let them cool fully, 15 minutes or so.

To help remove the pops, briefly submerge the molds in hot water. Quickly dip each side of the paletas in the coconut chips, pressing lightly so they stick, and serve right away. If the chips don't stick, you just need to melt the outsides a tiny bit more, so try a blowtorch (sure, okay, Edgar) or a couple seconds over a gas stovetop flame.

SALTED MASA CHOCOLATE-PECAN COOKIES

At Nixta, we've got a lot of masa around, so we end up playing with it, and not just for the dinner menu. Masa is right at home in sweets—in all manner of sweet tamales and atoles, like Champurrado (page 99), as well as in these chocolaty, pecan-laden cookies. Here its signature earthy quality tips the scale away from sugary in the same way salt would, which by the way we also sprinkle on top. Buy blue masa harina for the coolest colored cookies.

Take note that we freeze them before baking in order to prevent butter leakage and ensure they hit that perfect balance of chewy and a little crispy.

Equipment: stand mixer or handheld mixer

1 cup plus 2 tablespoons sugar
7 ounces (1¾ sticks) unsalted butter, at room temperature
2 eggs
1½ cups all-purpose flour
⅓ cup packed masa harina, preferably heirloom corn
¾ teaspoon baking powder
½ teaspoon Morton kosher salt
¼ teaspoon baking soda
½ cup semisweet baking chocolate chunks
½ cup chopped pecans
Flaky sea salt

Makes about 25 cookies

Get started on these cookies at least 4 hours before you plan to bake them.

In a stand mixer fitted with the whisk (or in a medium bowl with a handheld mixer), beat the sugar and butter on medium-high speed until light and fluffy, 1 to 2 minutes, scraping the sides of the bowl halfway through. Stop the mixer, then add the eggs and beat until well combined, about 2 minutes.

In a separate medium mixing bowl, whisk together the flour, masa harina, baking powder, salt, and baking soda. Add the flour mixture to the butter mixture and stir until smooth with no dry spots, scraping the bowl occasionally. Add the chocolate and pecans and mix to distribute evenly.

Try your best to avoid handling the dough much with your hands, which could warm up the butter. Line a sheet pan with parchment paper. Use a cookie scoop or spoon to scoop out balls (a generous 2 tablespoons per) and transfer them to the lined pan in a single layer. Use your fingers to gently and slightly flatten them. Sprinkle on some sea salt.

Freeze uncovered for at least 4 hours before baking. (At this point, you can transfer them to an airtight container and freeze for up to 1 month. Don't thaw before baking.)

Preheat the oven to 375°F. Line a sheet pan with parchment paper.

Arrange cookies about 2 inches apart on the prepared sheet pan. Bake until golden all over, firm at the edges and a little soft in the center, 16 to 18 minutes, rotating the sheet pan halfway through.

Let the cookies cool in the sheet pan before eating.

MOCHI CHURROS

Japanese-Mexi Fried Dough

We first made this riff on the classic when we collaborated with Shion Aikawa, Austin's ramen trailblazer. Koda Farms Mochiko (sweet rice flour) in the dough gives the result an irresistible bouncy chew and adding Japanese sanshō (berries of the prickly ash tree) to the cinnamon sugar coating provides an unexpected citrusy, tingly lift.

Equipment: stand mixer, piping bag with ¾- to 1-inch star tip or a churro-maker machine (lol, since you have one), deep-fry thermometer

BATTER

1¼ cups water
1 teaspoon demerara or granulated sugar
¾ teaspoon Morton kosher salt
1½ cups Koda Farms mochiko (sweet rice flour)
⅔ cup fine cornmeal
2 tablespoons neutral oil, such as grapeseed or canola
2 eggs, lightly beaten

CHURROS

Neutral oil, such as grapeseed or canola, for deep-frying (about 3 quarts)
1 cup granulated sugar
3 tablespoons ground cinnamon
2 teaspoons finely ground sanshō pepper (optional but gooood)
Dulce de leche, for serving

Makes about 12 churros

MAKE THE BATTER: In a medium saucepan, bring the water to a boil. Add the demerara sugar and salt and stir until the sugar dissolves. Stir in the flour and cornmeal, turn off the heat, then transfer to a stand mixer fitted with the paddle. Mix on medium-low speed to make a thick-ass dough. Let cool for 5 minutes.

Start mixing on low, then in a thin steady stream, pour in the oil. Next, add the eggs a third or so at a time, waiting until the previous dose of egg is well incorporated before adding more.

Transfer to a piping bag with a ¾- to 1-inch star tip or your churro-maker machine. Set aside while you heat the oil.

MAKE THE CHURROS: Pour 3 inches of oil into a large Dutch oven, and heat to 400°F.

In a large bowl, combine the granulated sugar, cinnamon, and sanshō pepper and stir well. Set a wire rack in a sheet pan and keep them near the stove.

Frying 3 churros at a time, pipe one 4- to 5-inch length of batter for each churro directly into the oil and fry, turning halfway through, until golden brown, 2 to 3 minutes.

Remove the churros from the oil, shaking off any excess, then add them directly to the cinnamon-sugar mix. Turn to coat them well, then arrange them on the wire rack while you fry and coat the rest the same way, letting the oil return to temp between batches. (Strain and keep the oil for future frying adventures.)

Serve hot with dulce de leche in a bowl for dipping.

"SHOLEH ZARD"

Persian-Mexi Rice Pudding

This is the story of how a bunch of Texans fell in love with a Persian dessert at a Mexican(ish) restaurant. During the to-go phase of the pandemic, we had to momentarily ditch our paletas (the stubborn lil' bastards melt!) and come up with a new dessert. Edgar had me taste an arroz con leche he'd been messing with. "This is great, but you know what would make it even better?" I said. "If it was sholeh zard." And thus, a food baby was born.

Maman has chosen to remind me practically every day that this isn't "real" sholeh zard. Maman Joon, if one of our most beloved dishes is wrong, I don't want to be right.

- 1 cup Carolina gold or Arborio rice, unrinsed
- 3 cups whole milk
- 1 cup heavy cream
- ½ cup sugar
- 1 tablespoon pure vanilla extract
- 1 cinnamon stick
- 1 cardamom pod, preferably black
- 1 tablespoon ground turmeric
- 1 tablespoon Saffron Water (it's easy—see page 19)
- ⅛ teaspoon Morton kosher salt
- 3 tablespoons cold unsalted butter, cut into 6 pieces
- 2 egg yolks
- 1 teaspoon ground cinnamon
- 1 cup (1 ounce) freeze-dried strawberries, finely ground
- ⅓ cup (3 ounces) finely chopped salted roasted pistachios
- Flaky sea salt, for sprinkling

Serves 4 to 6

Bring 6 cups of water to a hard boil in a 4- to 6-quart Dutch oven or other large pot over high heat. Add the rice and cook, stirring occasionally, until the grains begin to soften around the edges but are still raw in the middle, about 2 minutes. Drain the rice in a fine-mesh sieve, but don't rinse it.

Rinse the pot with cold water to cool it down, then pop it back over to the stove. In the rinsed pot, combine the milk, cream, sugar, vanilla, cinnamon stick, cardamom, turmeric, saffron water, and kosher salt. Set over medium heat and cook, stirring occasionally, until the sugar has dissolved and bubbles appear around the edge, about 15 minutes. Resist the urge to turn up the heat to make it boil faster. The goal is to let the spices slowly infuse the milk and cream for deep flavor.

Gently stir in the rice, making sure the grains are all well coated. Turn the heat down to low and very gently simmer, stirring gently a few times to make sure the grains don't stick to the bottom, until the mixture has the consistency of a loose pudding, 45 to 50 minutes. The liquid should be thick enough to coat the back of a spoon and the rice should be tender with a slight chew.

Add the butter two pieces at a time, stirring until fully melted after each addition. Remove from the heat and let cool until warm, stirring regularly, about 5 minutes. Stir in the egg yolks one at a time, fully incorporating the first before adding the second.

Transfer the sholeh zard to a large bowl. Let cool, then cover and refrigerate until fully chilled, at least 12 hours or up to 3 days. Fish out and discard the cinnamon stick and cardamom pod. (If you don't want to wait, fill another large bowl with very icy water, add the bowl with the sholeh zard, and stir gently but well occasionally, until chilled, about 30 minutes.)

Divide the sholeh zard among bowls. Dust each one with some of the ground cinnamon (add it to a fine mesh strainer, then tap-tap). Next, dust each one with the strawberry powder to cover the entire surface. Sprinkle on the pistachios, then some flaky sea salt, and serve.

SAFFRON TRES LECHES

Persian-Mexi Soaked Sponge Cake

A symbol of the Bigi and Rico union, this winner merges a big cozy hunk of Mexican tres leches cake with beguiling Persian spices, like saffron and cardamom. Ours is truly next level. We're out here using four milks, not just tres leches!

It's made in advance by design, so the cake can thoroughly suck up those leches. It's perfect for a dinner party. Just clear those plates, bust it out of the fridge, and take your bows.

Equipment: stand mixer or handheld mixer

CAKE

- Softened butter and all-purpose flour, for the pan
- ¾ cup whole milk
- 4 tablespoons (2 ounces/½ stick) unsalted butter, plus more for the pan
- 3 eggs
- 1¼ cups sugar
- 2 cups all-purpose flour, plus more for dusting
- 1½ teaspoons baking powder
- ½ teaspoon Morton kosher salt

SAFFRON LECHES

- 2 cups whole milk
- 1 teaspoon saffron threads, crushed
- 2 cardamom pods, preferably black
- 1 tablespoon ground turmeric
- 1 teaspoon Morton kosher salt
- One 14-ounce can sweetened condensed milk
- One 12-ounce can evaporated milk
- One 13.5-ounce can coconut milk, preferably Chaokoh

WHIPPED CREAM AND SERVING

- 3 cups heavy cream
- 3 tablespoons sugar
- 1 tablespoon ground turmeric
- ¼ teaspoon Morton kosher salt
- Chopped unsalted roasted pistachios, for garnish

Serves 12

MAKE THE CAKE: Preheat the oven to 375°F. Grease a 9 by 13-inch baking dish with butter and then sift on a thin layer of flour, knocking out the excess.

In a small saucepan, heat the milk and butter over medium heat just until the butter melts. Set aside off the heat.

In a stand mixer fitted with the whisk, beat the eggs on low speed. Add the sugar ¼ cup or so at a time on low speed, then increase to medium-high until pale and fluffy, about 3 minutes.

Remove the bowl from the mixer. Sift in the flour, baking powder, and salt and use a flexible spatula to gently fold until smooth with no dry spots. Add the warm milk mixture and stir just until smooth. Don't overmix.

Pour the batter into the prepared baking dish and smooth the top. Bake until the surface is golden and a toothpick inserted in the center comes out clean, 25 to 35 minutes, rotating the pan halfway through.

Let cool for 15 minutes, while you make the saffron leches.

MAKE THE SAFFRON LECHES: In a medium saucepan, combine the milk, saffron, cardamom, turmeric, and salt and heat over medium, stirring occasionally, until steaming but not bubbling, about 5 minutes. Remove from the heat, then stir in the condensed milk, evaporated milk, and coconut milk until smooth. Measure out 1½ cups of the milk mixture and put it in the fridge to chill for serving.

Use a toothpick or fork to poke holes all over the cooled cake, every ¼ inch or so. Pour the remaining warm milk mixture evenly over the cake. Let it cool completely.

Cover and refrigerate to chill the cake and let it absorb those leches, at least 12 hours or up to 3 days.

MAKE THE WHIPPED CREAM AND SERVE: In a stand mixer fitted with the whisk (or in a bowl with a handheld mixer), whip the cream, sugar, turmeric, and salt until soft peaks form. Chill until ready to use.

Cut the cake into 12 slices. Drizzle a spoonful of the reserved saffron milk onto plates, add the slices, and top with a dollop of the whipped cream and sprinkle of pistachios.

CORN FLAN WITH RUBY RED GRAPEFRUIT CARAMEL

Here at Nixta, we're rowdy about corn. Yeah, we make all that masa, but come summer, we also use fresh sweet corn like it's going out of style. Not even dessert is safe. For instance, we infuse corn's magic into a velvety Mexican-style flan to give it a seductive savory dimension. Then we add a Texas touch with a little Ruby Red grapefruit in the caramel and fresh juicy segments on top.

Equipment: 6 to 8 ramekins (about 6 ounces each)

GRAPEFRUIT CARAMEL

1 tablespoon Ruby Red grapefruit zest
½ cup Ruby Red grapefruit juice (1 to 2 grapefruits)
¾ cup sugar
1 tablespoon water
½ teaspoon Morton kosher salt

FLAN

2 cups corn kernels
1¼ cups whole milk
1 cup heavy cream
⅔ cup sugar
½ teaspoon Morton kosher salt
1 vanilla bean, split lengthwise
4 eggs
2 egg yolks

FOR SERVING

2 Ruby Red grapefruits, supremed (look it up)
Flaky sea salt

Serves 6 to 8

MAKE THE GRAPEFRUIT CARAMEL: Set out six to eight 6-ounce ramekins. In a small bowl, stir together the grapefruit zest and juice.

To a small saucepan, add the sugar, water, and salt, but don't stir. Set the pan over medium heat and cook without stirring until it melts and bubbles, about 5 minutes. Keep cooking, swirling the pan, until the color is deep golden, about 5 minutes more. Carefully add the grapefruit juice mixture (it will bubble vigorously), turn the heat to low, and whisk until smooth. Immediately pour the caramel into the ramekins. Set aside to let the caramel set for 1 hour. It won't get totally hard.

MAKE THE FLAN: In a blender, combine the corn, milk, and cream and blend on high until smooth, 30 to 45 seconds. Strain through a fine-mesh sieve into a medium saucepan, pressing on and then discarding the solids.

Add the sugar and salt. Scrape the vanilla seeds into the pan and add the pod. Set over medium heat and bring to a gentle simmer, stirring, about 8 minutes. Remove the pan from the heat and let cool for a couple minutes. Discard the vanilla pod.

In a blender (or in a medium bowl with an immersion blender), blend the whole eggs and egg yolks until well combined but no more than a little frothy. If necessary, transfer to a medium bowl. While whisking constantly to avoid scrambling, pour into the corn mixture in a thin, steady stream.

Immediately and tenderly, divide the mixture among the caramel-lined ramekins. Tap each gently against the counter to remove air bubbles.

Preheat the oven to 325°F.

Arrange the ramekins in a deep baking dish with some space between them. Pour in enough hot but not boiling water to the pan to come halfway up the sides of the ramekins.

Cover the baking dish loosely with foil and bake until the flan is just set with a slight jiggle in the center, 40 to 45 minutes.

Carefully remove the hot ramekins and let cool to room temperature, about 45 minutes. Cover and refrigerate for at least 4 hours or up to 3 days.

TO SERVE: Run a thin knife around the edges of each ramekin. Invert onto a plate, allowing the grapefruit caramel to flow over the flan. Garnish with the supremed grapefruits and a sprinkle of sea salt.

BEANS, DRESSING, HOT SAUCE, AND STUFF

CHIPOTLE MAYO

This is one of only a few ways to improve on Duke's mayo. Canned chipotles add that smoke and spice and lime brightens it all up. To make it extra fancy, call it "chipotle aioli" and pretend you crafted it and didn't just throw a few ingredients in a blender.

2 cups mayo (Duke's!)
2 tablespoons fresh lime juice
1¼ teaspoons Morton kosher salt, plus more to taste
One 3.7-ounce can chipotle chiles in adobo sauce

Makes about 2½ cups

Dump it all in a blender and blend, stirring and scraping the sides if necessary, until completely smooth (no more seeds!), about 2 minutes. Season to taste with salt. (Keeps in the fridge for up to 2 weeks.)

NIXTA'S FRESNO HOT SAUCE

Whiz chiles with vinegar, salt, and sugar and you've got tasty hot sauce. But let those chiles hang and brew for 2 weeks first and you've got something truly special: tangy, complex, and full of umami. We use Fresnos, but this recipe works with any chiles you like. Use sriracha instead of hot sauce if you're lazy.

WORD OF WARNING: When you clean up after making this, open your windows; the air will get a little tear-gassy because of those chiles.

1 cup plus 1 tablespoon demerara or granulated sugar
1 cup red wine vinegar
2 tablespoons Morton kosher salt
1 pound Fresno chiles, stemmed and thinly sliced
3 garlic cloves, peeled but whole

Makes about 3½ cups

In a 1-quart glass jar, combine the sugar, vinegar, and salt and stir well to mostly dissolve the sugar. Add the chiles and garlic, then press down so they're submerged in the liquid. If necessary, put a piece of plastic wrap on the surface and add a weight to keep them submerged.

Cover with an airtight lid and keep the jar in a dark place, like the cupboard or above the fridge, for 2 weeks. No stirring or burping needed.

Blend on high speed until completely smooth, 2 to 3 minutes. Strain if you want to remove any lingering seeds. (Keeps in the fridge for up to 1 month.)

PILONCILLO DRESSING

Mexi Nuoc Cham

The sugar is Mexican, the flavors are Vietnamese nuoc cham with a smidge of Frenchy vinaigrette. The effect is glorious, whether it's rallying greens salads, glazing up chicken wings, or balancing the rich, buttery slices of fish on Hamachi Tostadas (page 214).

2 ounces piloncillo (see page 18) or palm sugar, bashed into several pieces (⅓ cup)
Finely grated zest of 3 limes
¾ cup fresh lime juice (6 to 7 limes)
¼ cup fish sauce (we like Squid brand)
¼ cup finely chopped shallot

Makes about 1¼ cups

In a blender, combine the piloncillo, lime zest, lime juice, and fish sauce and blend until the sugar has completely dissolved, about 2 minutes. Pour it into a container and stir in the shallots.

Before serving, let it hang at room temp for at least 30 minutes or even better, refrigerate overnight. (Keeps in the fridge for up to 2 days.)

PUFFED AMARANTH

There is life before discovering puffed amaranth. Then there's life in its glorious wake. A hot pan, a few minutes of shake-shaky, and pop-pop-pop! You've got a crispy, airy, buttery sprinkle for snacking or topping anything from our Carrot Tostadas (page 218) and Space Glizzies (page 206) to your fave salad.

¼ cup amaranth

Makes about ¾ cup

Heat a dry medium skillet over medium-high for 3 to 4 minutes. To test if it's hot enough, add a little drop of water. If it sizzles and evaporates instantly, it's ready.

Add the amaranth and a tight-fitting lid and shake constantly and vigorously for 1 to 2 minutes, until at least 80 percent of the grains have turned from golden to white. That means they've puffed!

Transfer to a plate or shallow bowl to cool. (Keeps in an airtight container at room temp for up to 1 month.)

DUCK-FAT REFRIED BEANS

Refried beans is a food born of necessity, a way to turn leftovers into something novel. Our duck-fat refrieds? Born of a different kind of necessity: What to do with all the fat remaining after we make duck carnitas! Instead of throwing out that liquid gold and then turning around to buy pork lard for our beans, we tried swapping it out one day. I swear, it felt like an Isaac Newton–level discovery. Needless to say, we never went back.

You won't ever be sad to have some on hand, whether you're making Migas Tacos (page 190) or Bean and Cheese Tacos (page 222), Huevos Rancheros (page 42), or Enfrijoladas (page 50), where the beans become a silky sauce (so don't toss the bean cooking liquid!). And while the extra-flavorful leftover fat from duck carnitas is what shoots this into the stratosphere, store-bought duck fat works fine.

- 1 pound dried black beans, soaked in water overnight (see Note)
- ¾ cup rendered duck fat, preferably from duck carnitas (see page 225)
- 1 medium yellow onion, cut into ½-inch dice
- 1 small garlic clove, peeled but whole
- 1¼ teaspoons ground cumin
- Scant ½ teaspoon ground cinnamon
- 1 tablespoon Morton kosher salt, plus more to taste

Makes about 5 cups

Drain and rinse the beans.

Heat 3 tablespoons of the duck fat in a 5- to 6-quart Dutch oven over medium. Add the onion and garlic and sauté until the onions soften, about 3 minutes. Add the cumin and cinnamon and stir for 2 minutes, just to bring out the aromas.

Add the beans and enough water to cover by 1 inch, then crank the heat to bring to a boil. Lower the heat to cook at a gentle simmer, stirring occasionally, until the beans are tender and creamy but still intact, 1 to 1½ hours, topping up with hot water to keep the beans submerged, if necessary.

Drain the solids in a large sieve set over a bowl, reserving the liquid. Return the solids to the pot, add the remaining 9 tablespoons duck fat and the salt, then use an immersion blender (a stand blender works, too, though you might have to stir and scrape) to blend until smooth. If necessary, gradually add some of the reserved cooking liquid until you have a thick but pourable situation. Season with more salt to taste.

They're ready to eat! (Keeps in the fridge for up to 5 days or in the freezer for up to 3 months. The remaining bean cooking liquid keeps, separately, for up to 5 days.)

NOTE: Follow your bean mood and use the best, freshest dried beans you can find. Yeah, you heard me: *Fresh* dried beans, aka beans that have been harvested and dried recently and haven't been sitting on a store shelf for lord knows how long. (Those take forever to cook and sometimes I'm convinced they never get fully creamy.) Companies that sell heirloom beans typically fit the bill and let you choose from a whole-ass spectrum of colors, all of which have slightly different flavors. Black beans are fab here, but please feel free to go wild. To use canned black beans, drain and rinse five 15-ounce cans, add them after cooking the onions, then proceed, simmering for 5 minutes instead of 1 hour.

ACKNOWLEDGMENTS

FROM SASA

This book exists because a number of very talented people showed up and continued to believe in us even when we were tired, covered in salsa, and perpetually saying "Pardon the delay."

To my parents, Ghamar (aka Maman) and Farhard (aka Baba) Mardanbigi. Thank you for raising me with strong values, strong opinions, a penchant for asking for a deeper discount from the manager, and the confidence to believe I could do something wildly impractical (like write a cookbook). You taught me that hard work is non-negotiable, the most powerful thing is my mind, and that quitting is not an option. Every page carries your love, your sacrifices, and probably your voice in my head asking why I haven't eaten more.

To my siblings, Maryam, the snack-master and our resident crybaby; Mona, my trauma-bonded canary bird roomie; Mohamad, baby bro, elite travel partner, and my grumpy twin; and Makayla and Layla, who are part of this big, silly, ever-evolving story. You all are deeply annoying at times—and completely irreplaceable. I love you more than I will ever admit in the group chat (that I will respond to in 3 weeks).

To my boo, partner, and co-conspirator, Edgar Rico aka Gargar—the reason I'm not a total Type A psycho 24/7 and the person who can somehow still make me laugh in the middle of chaos with a cute lil' whistle. Thank you for dreaming with me, building something through exhaustion, and believing that this story was worth telling even when it felt impossible. I'd do it all again with you (after a longgggggggg coma nap).

To our coauthor, JJ Goode, whom we trusted to guide us through the madness of cookbook writing. Thank you for your weirdo humor, ability to crawl into our brains, and uncanny ability for knowing exactly when to rein us in and when to let us cook (literally and figuratively). This book is better because of you.

To our photographer (and dear friend), Mackenzie (aka Mack) Smith, whose photographs go beyond what's on the plate. Thank you for *seeing* us and for making even the messiest days look beautiful—from literal day one many years ago. Your words of encouragement and ability to pull us out of some dark moments went above and beyond what we could have asked for. These photos tell the story better than we ever could.

To Claudia Gizell Aparicio Gamundi, our unofficial brand and creative director since before Day 1, and the chaotic genius sometimes known as Pinche Juan. Thank you for shaping Nixta from pure instinct—and for casually creating the hand-drawn typeface on this book cover like it was no big deal. We love you so much.

To our editor, Claire Yee, who somehow saw the vision years ago (when we weren't quite ready) and thankfully never gave up her pursuit. She brought CLAIRity (dad joke!) and calm to a process that is neither of those things by nature. Thank you for your sharp eye, patience, and for helping us turn a thousand ideas into something real and meaningful. And to the rest of the Ten Speed book squad: Lizzie Allen, Liana Parry Faughnan, Kristin Sargianis, Serena Sigona, Mari Gill, Faith Hague, Joey Lozada, and David Hawk.

To our literary agent, Kim Witherspoon, who believed in this book early, fought for it fiercely, and expertly guided us through the parts of publishing that feel like a secret maze. Thank you for your wisdom, your advocacy, and for always making us feel protected, supported, and slightly more confident than we probably should be.

To our recipe tester, Farideh Sadeghin—fellow Persian and elite snack master. Thank you for your sound advice and for putting care into these recipes as if they were your own. On that note, I will never tell your baba you preferred our Khoresht Karafs recipe to his—c'mon. On another random note, one day we *will* launch Sidekick, the app where women can temporarily abandon (aka *kick* out) their often boring boyfriends/husbands on vacations to hang out with more interesting people. Can't wait to dominate the tech space alongside you as my founding partner.

To lil' Sasa of yesteryear—mushroom haircut queen and panda sweater enthusiast. Thank you for never giving up, even when you had absolutely no idea what you were not giving up on. You remind me why rooting for yourself matters, why creativity matters, and why it's okay to keep going even when I feel small. You carried this book (and me) spiritually, whether you knew it or not. This is for us!

And, finally, to everyone who has ever cheered us on or believed in what we're building by showing up and pulling up a chair. We couldn't have done this without you.

FROM GARGAR

To the community of Austin and beyond, which helped to shape Nixta into the special place it is today. To the familiar faces we see week after week, to our regulars, and to the families we've watched grow alongside us (and their babies, who end up covered in beans). Thank you for trusting us, feeding your families with us, and letting Nixta be part of your lives. And to everyone who continues to show up and support this project on Dozen Street in Austin: Your belief, your energy, and your presence made all of this possible. We love you.

To every single team member, past and present, at Nixta: This book wouldn't have been possible without you. Nixta is truly nothing without the people who show up every day with so much pride, silliness, and the crazy faith that this thing we made is worth it. Every service, every prep day, every late night, and every moment of intention you've poured into this place is what made it special. This story exists because of you. I'm endlessly grateful to each and every one of you.

To my parents, Fermin and Flor: Thank you for your selflessness and for having the courage to leave everything you knew to build a life in this country. Your journey to America was the foundation of everything I do. Every step I've taken has been with the hope that I could make you proud. This book is proof that your sacrifices were worth it and that your story deserves to be shared.

To all of my previous chefs and mentors who showed up for me along the way: Thank you for teaching me how to navigate the chaotic, demanding, and beautiful world of restaurants. You showed me the way—sometimes through patience, sometimes through pressure—and those lessons shaped how I cook, how I lead, and how I show up every day.

And finally, to my wife, Sara Mardanbigi aka Sasa: Thank you for believing in me when I didn't fully believe in myself, for pushing me to be better, and for grounding me through every high and low. Thank you for building something beautiful with me, side by side. And after all the love, care, and work you have poured into making our business and our lives so full, I owe you a lifetime supply of gratitude, admiration, and at least one very solid foot massage, redeemable at any time.

BABY SARA

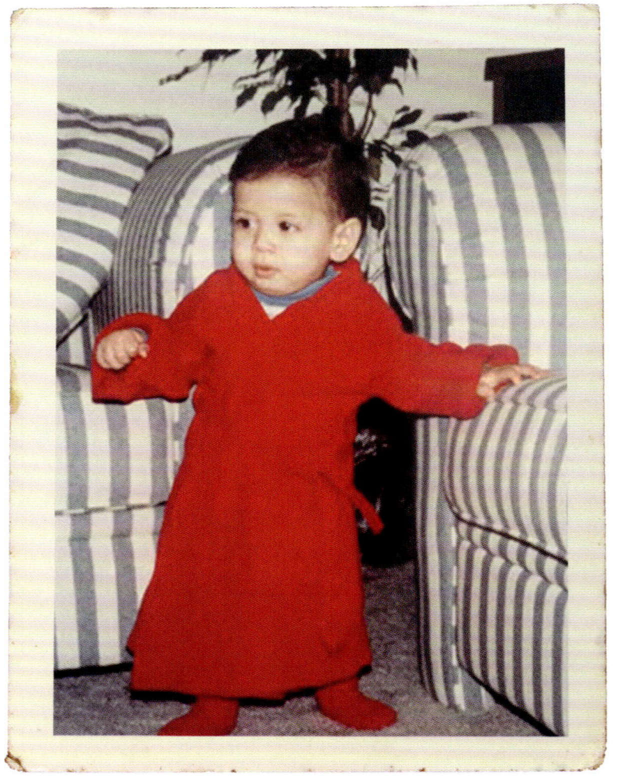

BABY EDGAR

ABOUT THE CONTRIBUTORS

SARA MARDANBIGI is the co-owner of the Michelin Bib Gourmand and James Beard Award–winning Nixta Taqueria and the CEO of Taking the Joke Waaaay Too Far. She is an Iranian-American creative, a community builder, and the leader of Nixta's operations—including business development, strategic partnerships, people management, content and marketing, and mostly just picking up trash as Nixta's senior (not tenured; just old) custodian. This cookbook is her attempt to bottle the Nixta magic, while sparing you the stress dreams, teeth grinding, and broken water pipes it took to make it happen.

EDGAR RICO is the co-owner of Nixta Taqueria and the CEO of Narcolepsy. (Seriously, he can fall asleep anywhere in seconds.) He's a Mexican-American chef, a James Beard Award winner, a *Time* 100 Next recipient, a *Food & Wine* Best New Chef, a winner of *Food & Wine*'s Best New Restaurant, an American Culinary Corps ambassador for the U.S. State Department, and a proud World Central Kitchen member. (Award for the most amount of awards.) His creative method is equal parts ancestral wisdom and I-had-a-vision-at-3-a.m. energy. This cookbook is his tribute to the people and foods that shaped him—and to everyone who's ever trusted him when he said, "Just taste this, you're gonna love it."

JJ GOODE helps people write books, and mostly cookbooks, which are the best books. He loves working with Sasa and Gargar, who are the best people.

MACKENZIE SMITH is an Austin- and NYC-based photographer who fell headfirst into Nixta's orbit and never looked back. Her work lives at the intersection of food, people, and place—capturing moments that feel lived-in, joyful, and deeply human. For this book, Mack photographed the food, the hands, and the beautiful chaos, doing her best to keep salsa and tahdig off her camera (she did not, ha). The cherry on top was meeting Sasa and Gargar's families—and getting the chance to thank them for raising two of earth's best.

INDEX

D

V

W

Y

Z

TEN SPEED PRESS
An imprint of the Crown Publishing Group
A division of Penguin Random House LLC
1745 Broadway
New York, NY 10019
tenspeed.com
penguinrandomhouse.com

Typefaces: HAL's Timezone and Dinamo's Marfa

Library of Congress Cataloging-in-Publication Data
Names: Mardanbigi, Sara, 1988– (author) | Rico, Edgar, 1989– (author)
Title: Nixta taqueria presents from tacos to tahdig: recipes and stories from Mexico, Iran, and the in-between / by Sara Mardanbigi and Edgar Rico.
Identifiers: LCCN 2026005601 (print) | LCCN 2026005602 (ebook) | ISBN 9780593838778 hardcover | ISBN 9780593838785 ebook
Subjects: LCSH: International cooking | Cooking, Iranian | Cooking, Mexican | LCGFT: Cookbooks
Classification: LCC TX725.A1 M3468 2026 (print) | LCC TX725.A1 (ebook) | DDC 641.59—dc23/eng/20260211
LC record available at https://lccn.loc.gov/2026005601
LC ebook record available at https://lccn.loc.gov/2026005602

Hardcover ISBN 978-0-593-83877-8
Ebook ISBN 978-0-593-83878-5

Editor: Claire Yee | Production editor: Liana Faughnan
Designer: Lizzie Allen | Production designers: Mari Gill and Faith Hague
Production: Serena Sigona | Prepress color managers: Nick Patton and Hannah Hunt
Food and prop stylist: Alicia Mendez-Clayton | Food and prop stylist assistant: Sunnie Reagin
Photo assistant: Janai Cano
Copy editor: Kate Slate | Proofreaders: Eldes Tran, Sigi Nacson, and Miriam Taveras
Compositor: Hannah Hunt | Indexer: Eldes Tran
Publicist: David Hawk | Marketer: Joey Lozada

Manufactured in China

10 9 8 7 6 5 4 3 2 1

First Edition

"Every time I touch down in Austin, I make it a point to go to Nixta. The food is consistently exciting, comforting, and delicious; only humans as wonderful as Edgar and Sara could have re-created that so beautifully in print with *Nixta Taqueria Presents: From Tacos to Tahdig*."

—**MADISON McFERRIN,**
singer, songwriter, and producer

"To say Nixta Taqueria is a culinary haven isn't an exaggeration—it is simply accurate. It's the rare place where 'food for the soul' doesn't feel like a slogan but a side effect. Every bite feels unmistakably like Sara and Edgar: bright, generous, unfussy, and quietly dazzling—nothing overworked, nothing hiding behind tricks. A feast for the eyes and a treat for the belly. We are ridiculously lucky to get a window into this magical duo's recipes and stories—because that's what a great recipe really is: a story you can taste and try to retell in your own kitchen, usually with one missing ingredient, one extra splash of something, and that giddy feeling that comes with sharing a great meal with people you love."

—**CARLA GUGINO,**
actress and Nixta Taqueria devotee

"Nixta Taqueria manages to somehow be simultaneously down home and traditional yet completely forward thinking at the same time. The food is rooted in Mexican cooking with a healthy dash of Persian influence, and it has been one of my favorite restaurants in the world since falling in love with it years ago. The idea that their recipes can be enjoyed by anyone through this book is incredible!"

—**ADRIAN QUESADA,**
musician and producer